Seasons of the Spirit

*Scriptural Reflections for
Advent, Christmas, Lent and Easter*

By

LeRoy Clementich, C.S.C.

Corby Books
Notre Dame, IN

SEASONS OF THE SPIRIT

SEASONS OF THE SPIRIT
Scriptural Reflections for
Advent, Christmas, Lent and Easter

Copyright © 2011 by LeRoy Clementich

All rights reserved.
No part of this book may be used
or reproduced in any manner whatsoever
without the expressed permission on the publisher.

10 9 8 7 6 5 4 3 2

ISBN 978-0-9833586-0-2

Published by
CORBY BOOKS
A Division of Corby Publishing, LP
P.O. Box 93
Notre Dame, IN 46556
1961 Tyler Rd.
Lakeville, IN 46536
www.corbypublishing.com

Manufactured in the United States of America

Table of Contents

    Introduction vii
    Acknowledgments xi
    Preface xiii
1 First Sunday of Advent 1
2 Second Sunday of Advent 13
3 Third Sunday of Advent 25
4 Fourth Sunday of Advent 37
5 Christmas 47
6 The Holy Family 51
7 Mary, Mother of God 59
8 Epiphany 63
9 Baptism of the Lord 67
10 First Sunday of Lent 77
11 Second Sunday of Lent 87
12 Third Sunday of Lent 99
13 Fourth Sunday of Lent 111
14 Fifth Sunday of Lent 123
15 Palm Sunday 135
16 Holy Thursday 145
17 Easter 149
18 Second Sunday of Easter 159

19	Third Sunday of Easter 171
20	Fourth Sunday of Easter 181
21	Fifth Sunday of Easter 191
22	Sixth Sunday of Easter 203
23	Ascension of the Lord 215
24	Solemnity of Pentecost 225
25	Holy Trinity 237
26	Corpus Christi 241
27	Epilogue: The Church at Prayer 245

Introduction

The author of this book has many skills, but the ability to recognize his own enormous talent in the realm of human communication is not one of them. Even though he's been named the best Scripture columnist in the U.S. and Canada four times; and even though he was always the Archbishop's go-to guy when a controversial message regarding the liturgy needed to be communicated to the faithful; and even though his friends, yours truly included, stopped by his office to chat so often that he sometimes had to hole up in his tiny apartment to get any work done; still, given all that, when he called to tell me about this book deal he added: "I'm not sure why they want to do it, but they do, can you believe that?"

Fortunately Father LeRoy Clementich, "Clem" to everyone he's ever met, makes up for his impenetrable humility by being willing to try pretty much anything that would help the person requesting it. I learned that about him in 1998, shortly after accepting the job as editor of the Anchorage Archdiocese's newspaper—a newspaper that didn't exist yet.

My new boss, Archbishop Francis T. Hurley, a man of great courage and action and no excuses, wanted the paper to be more than Bible crosswords, First Communion photos and notices of spaghetti dinners. He wanted it to be an instrument that would help his people act and think and live in the world as Catholics, and maybe turn a few not-yet-Catholic heads as well. A few days into my new job, the archbishop walked in with an especially twinkly twinkle in his bright Irish eyes: "We need someone who can help people prepare to receive the Word by sharing a thoughtful reflection on the upcoming Sunday Readings," he announced. "And I know who can do it: Clem."

Not that Clem himself had any inkling that he could do it. He'd been preparing homilies for more than forty years at that point, but he'd never thought about writing them down for publication. But asking was all it took for him to give it a whirl. Immediately, he opened his liturgical calendar and fed some paper into his enormous brown electric typewriter. He pecked out four 1500-word essays on the coming weeks' readings. "Take a look, John," he said, handing me the sheaf of neatly double-spaced pages. "Don't know if it's what you're looking for, but it's what I came up with."

I don't remember particulars of those first columns, but I do remember starting to grin about halfway through the first one and feeling the urge to shout "Yes!" by the time I had finished them all. The man could write! At least that part of the newspaper would be top notch, as the archbishop had predicted.

Clem's column became a popular item right out of the gate. Once in a while, maybe once a year, the column generated a feisty call or letter from someone who thought it too soft or too loving. I think someone actually wrote that once! But mostly inspired gratitude from readers who found new meaning in a Scripture passage or their own life after reading "Clem."

I'll never forget the first time I came back from the Catholic Press Association annual convention with Clem's first place award (a novelty that eventually wore off when he kept winning year after year). I said nothing and handed the plaque to him as he sat eating smoked salmon and Ritz crackers at his desk in the newspaper office. He was dumbfounded. I explained that his column had won first place, nationwide, going up against big names at big newspapers across the country. "I just can't believe it," he kept saying. Believe it.

Clem is a pleasure to read for many reasons. He has (1) a curious and sensitive outlook as the oldest of eight children raised on a North Dakota farm in the 1920s and 1930s; (2) a deep spiritual sense that defines the shades and edges of every experience because of having been brought up in a loving Catholic home, majoring in philosophy, serving in World War II, teaching theology for twenty years, and attending daily Mass pretty much since high school; (3) a taste for adventure (flying his little Cessna out across vast and unforgiving Alaska to celebrate Mass in isolated villages); and (4) a memory like the Library of Congress, comprehensive and organized. Plus, he's been alive a l-o-o-ong time, so his memories and stories are as plentiful as they are interesting. But what sets him apart from all the other interesting, thoughtful, adventurous octogenarians with tack-sharp memories and Catholicism deep in their bones is that thing I discovered the first time I read his work in Anchorage. He is a masterful storyteller. He has the rare ability to convey deep insights about the Gospels in a humble, personal, conversational style that makes it feel as though he were sitting across the table from you after Mass, sipping coffee and chewing the fat. You don't feel like you just read someone's Ph.D. dissertation, even though every word is anchored in sound theology. You don't feel preached to, even though you may be inspired to live better. If your experience is like mine, you feel like you just spent an hour with a God whisperer, a man who reads the Word like a composer reads music. You feel like you've sat with a wise old soul who has traveled the Gospels his entire long life, and traveled the Earth with equal excitement, curiosity, and openness to being transformed by what he encounters.

Clem has wandered long with the Word. The Gospel characters and messages remain his lifelong travel companions. And now in his 80s, he has learned to be still and let the Word wander through the vault of his memories, and to take note where the Word of God pauses. Back in the light of day, he shared those notes with us, clacking them down on his old computer in his tiny apartment—telling us stories of his journey with God.

John Roscoe

Acknowledgments

As in the professional careers of most people, success occurs at the hand and with the loving care of many people, some of whom have long since returned to the heart of God. I mention here only a few, but they are an important few.

The loving and patient Benedictine nun, teacher of English at St. Leo's High School, Minot, North Dakota. "You will be a writer," she once said, "if you ever learn how to spell." I did!

I cannot forget to acknowledge Notre Dame's well-beloved professor of modern literature, Frank O'Malley, who introduced me to the splendid works of modern Catholic authors.

And now a covey of individuals who encouraged me to write despite my misgivings: Brian Doyle, whose unique and incomparable style consistently brings joy to the heart; John Roscoe, my editor at the *Catholic Anchor* newspaper and my mentor, who gave me a start and the opportunity to see how writing really works; and to Joel Davidson who gave me support on days when writing did not come easily.

Father Carl Ebey will be happy to know that his apprehension about the Alaskan adventure was worth the risk. To him, eternal thanks.

To Archbishop Frank Hurley of Anchorage, Alaska, who

gave me the job that provided me with fifteen of the best and happiest years of my life, my deepest gratitude.

Nicholas Ayo, C.S.C., provided editorial assistance in the assembly of these writings.

Preface

I AM SURE THAT SOMEONE in the annals of writing must have commented on the fact (I believe it to be a fact) that many of the most critical episodes in one's lifetime seem to occur accidentally. It occurs to me, however, that we might as easily call these events "moments of grace."

Such was the case in my own regard when, back in another century, I received a phone call from my good friend, Francis Thomas Hurley, Archbishop of Anchorage, Alaska. I had made his acquaintance on several occasions while on fishing expeditions in the Great Land.

"Any chance," he asked, "that you could bring your Piper Cherokee up here and help us minister to Catholic folks who live in bush villages scattered around the Archdiocese?"

"Hey, that would be awesome," I replied, "but I seriously doubt whether my provincial superior would look kindly on such a proposal." He said: "Well, go ahead and ask him. He can only say no."

With some trepidation, therefore, I called Father Carl Ebey, my Provincial, and laid the request before him. His first question: "Are there any Catholics up there?" "Lots of them," I replied. "Well," he said, "I'll check with my Council and let you know." Six weeks later Father Ebey called back and said: "Okay, you can go up there for a few years, but if I ever need you here in Indiana, you will need to come back." Get this. I worked for Archbishop Francis Hurley for fifteen years, and Father Ebey never called back. Is that grace or what?

Truly, my years working for Archbishop Hurley were a blessing. I had the opportunity to fly into many small villages to celebrate the liturgy and bring the sacraments to welcoming Catholics.

In addition to my weekends in the bush, I held an office at the pastoral center in Anchorage where I served as a contact person for the Archbishop with the local lay parish administrators, answering questions and giving pastoral advice and encouragement.

The second Alaskan moment of grace came about with my introduction to John Roscoe, a young man who had only recently been hired as the first editor of *The Catholic Anchor*, the newspaper for the Archdiocese. Soon after taking over, he popped into my office one day and said: "Clem, I'm looking for someone to write a weekly article for the *Anchor*, a short commentary on the Sunday Scriptures that people can reflect on before heading off for Mass each weekend. It might help the folks get a head start on their pastor's Sunday homily. Do you think you could handle something like that?"

"Well," I said, "I have never written for a newspaper before, but I think that's a great idea. I'll give it my best shot." So that is how my public writing career began. Week after week I managed to beat the deadline and produce something folks of the Archdiocese gradually came to like. Many people years wrote to the editor saying that their Sunday experience at the liturgy was helped immensely by getting an early peek at what the Scriptures might be saying for that day.

The National Catholic Press Association also seemed to like what I wrote. They awarded me a First Place in Scripture Commentary on five different occasions.

I know that John and his able successor, Joel Davidson, were delighted to see that a limited circulation Catholic newspaper like the *Anchor* could compete with the "big boys" in New York, Chicago, and Los Angeles.

And so that, in part, is how the essays that you are about to read from week to week came to be. In the process of writing those pieces, a line from Georges Bernanos' *Diary of a Country Priest* often came to mind. The young parish priest who felt that he had never done anything well during his entire life is now close to death. A friend who had once shared his ministry is consoling him. "My only wish is that I could have brought you the oils of healing," said the former priest. His dying friend's last words were these: "It does not matter, my friend, grace is everywhere."

Yes, I have found it to be so. Grace can be found in the most unexpected moments of one's life. Isn't that amazing?

LeRoy Clementich, C.S.C.

A Note to the Reader

The reflections presented here are not homilies,
but they are reflections upon
the scriptural readings for the Sundays of
the seasons of Advent, Christmas, Lent and Easter
in each of the three liturgical cycles.

The Roman Catholic Mass Lectionary,
which contains the readings for each Sunday of the year,
is organized into three-year cycles of readings.
The years are designated A, B, or C.
Each yearly cycle begins on the first Sunday of Advent
(the last Sunday of November or first Sunday of December).
Year B follows Year A, Year C follows Year B,
then back again to A.
We are currently (November 28, 2010) in Year A
(The Gospel of St. Matthew).

Year A: Gospel of Matthew (November 2010 through 2011)
Year B: Gospel of Mark (December 2011 through 2012)
Year C: Gospel of Luke (December 2012 through 2013)

The Gospel of John is read throughout Easter, and is used
for other liturgical seasons including
Advent, Christmas, and Lent where appropriate.

1

First Sunday of Advent

†

YEAR A

EACH YEAR, PRECISELY ON THE First Sunday of Advent, I send out my yearly Christmas letter to the people who have been part of my life over these many years. Like many others who send Christmas greetings, I recite the usual interesting events that have occurred in my life during the past twelve months. In my most recent letter I began by expressing my amazement at how quickly the current year had passed. "Hey, didn't I just do this a little while ago?" I asked. Then I usually end the letter by saying, "Talk to you again next year." That is obviously a bit of hubris. Who knows whether I will still be here to do all this again next year? Twelve months is a lot of time.

However we choose to define it, time seems to be one of those elusive entities that continues going on around us while we are trying to do something that will give meaning to our lives. "The time you enjoy wasting is not wasted."

It is also interesting, at least to me, that we do not think much about time until it has suddenly come to an end for us: end of the day, end of the month, end of the year, yes, even the end of life. Then all of a sudden we ask, "Where did the time go?" End times are always a wakeup call for us in the sense that we realize that we cannot have that time segment of our life back again, ever.

Most Christians realize also that there is an end point in the liturgical year, the ecclesiastical year, the year of grace. It usually occurs around the end of the month of November, and it is titled, the "Thirty-fourth Sunday in Ordinary Time." It just happens that the Feast of Christ the King is also celebrated on that Sunday. In less than a week after that, we begin a new liturgical year with the First Sunday of Advent.

In some sense, the ending of one year of grace should not cause us anxiety, because there are no breaks in this year and no gaps. The life of Christ that is celebrated in the Church is truly unending. That does not mean that divine time simply goes around and around endlessly in a circle, like a merry-go-round. No, rather divine time is like a rising and a falling; indeed, all life in the cosmos is constantly in the process of death and resurrection.

So, then, what do we Christians celebrate with the oncoming of the First Sunday of Advent? Interestingly, Advent is both a beginning and an ending. It includes within itself the end of the secular year and the beginning of the Church's cycle. Within that great cycle are included all the great feasts of the Church's calendar: Christmas, of course, is one, but also the Paschal Mystery—that is, the suffering, death and resurrection of the Lord Jesus Christ.

For many Christians in past times, Advent was simply understood as a four-week introduction to the feast of Christmas. We must insist, however, that Advent holds a privileged position of its own. It is a time of anticipation and a time of waiting, not for the coming of the "baby Jesus," but rather an anticipation of Christ's continual coming through his death and resurrection.

So, then, how should the Christian consider the times in which we live? I think of it this way: Life is not merely a putting up with the vagaries of everyday existence, not just getting along as best we can with the time that is available to us. I think of life as pregnant with God, filled with the sacred, with the beautiful, the inexpressible. In short, every moment of our life is grace, a never-ending fountain of God's love for us. In that sense, therefore, we need not have any fear that we will "run out of time." God's gift of time is eternity happening just now.

The Scriptures:
Isaiah 2:1-5; Romans 13:11-14;
Matthew 24:37-44

Year B

Like most folks, I am not particularly worried or concerned about time. "There will always be time," I say. Perhaps I should be concerned, of course, because I'm always behind, behind time that is. But twice each year I do get a little concerned about time. Because I am a Catholic and I follow the liturgical calendar, I pay special attention to the First Sunday of Advent, the beginning of a new liturgical year, a year of grace. The second date or event I get concerned about is January 1, the beginning of the secular year. Both of these dates obviously have something to do with what we call time. Oddly enough, time does not exist as a distinct entity like, say, this computer I am presently pounding away at. I took the occasion, therefore, to look up the word "time" in *Webster's International Dictionary*, and, surprisingly, I found one entire column dedicated to time. That tells me that time, whether it exists or not, must play some part in our daily life. Webster simply defines it as "an interval between two events." Perhaps we should say that we all think we know what time is, because we experience it in various ways in our daily life whether we can define it or not.

Think of the words or phrases we ordinarily use to talk about time. Frequently during the day we ask, "Hey, what time is it?" The prison system talks about "doing time" or "serving time." We say: "We are either ahead of time or behind time." We keep time or we lose time. We save time or we waste time. We invest time and we manage time. Unfortunately, we also kill time! We say, "Time is money." A long time ago there used to be a radio program called "Time Marches On." We make time and save time. Many of us look for the "opportune time" to do something. Kindergarten teachers tell their students that they may go to the bathroom "one at a time." We speak of "having the time of our lives." The Scriptures speak of "a time to live and a time to die." All of us appreciate "quality time" with another person rather than simply "putting in time." Kids talk about "having a good time." During "work time" we are on the job; on weekends we look forward to "leisure time." Musicians talk about "keeping time" with their foot!

Anyone who has ever taken a timed exam knows what it means when the proctor says: "Time's up." We worry about running against time. All of us (particularly newspaper people) dread time-lines and deadlines. We don't like to be labeled being "behind the times" or out of date. For working people (and we are all working people) there is always concern about the time card or the time clock. Young lovers say that "time stands still when they are together." Sadly, for many people who are elderly, we say "time is getting short." When the thirty-first day of December or the Thirty-fourth Sunday in Ordinary Time rolls around, we know we've run out of time, at least for this year.

All of these references to time have at least one thing in common. They all are measured by a clock or a calendar: 24/7/365, as the phrase is used by many today. So, we say these moments have to do with "chronological time." It's a Greek word which means that we try to arrange events in an orderly fashion. It is simply a way for us to keep from getting lost in the universe!

But the ancient Greeks who always were looking for the meaning in things also have another word for time, which we Christians have adopted. It's simply called *kairos*. It's not a word that is ordinarily used except by liturgists and theologians. Actually, I could not even find it in *Webster's International Dictionary*!

The difference between *chronos* and *kairos* is that chronological time is linear, that is, it begins at a certain point and ends at another point. Chronos time says: "When something is over, it is over. Period! When you are out of time, you are out of time." Chronological time is always predictable. We keep time accurately. But chronological time actually has no meaning of itself. Every minute, every second is exactly like the minute or second that preceded it or which will follow it. It just keeps on ticking whether we think we can do something about it or not. Kairos time, however, is thought of as circular, going around and around. Kairos time is repeatable, even reversible. In other words, if you are using kairos time (as every Christian should) you can start over; for the Christian, it's never too late. We are never purely out of time, period! That is why kairos is called God-time or sacred time, time filled with mystery and with meaning.

That is also why, for instance, even though we Christians follow a chronological calendar, we also talk about a calendar year of grace, a year filled with God's grace, God's gifts. Did you ever notice how often our Sunday gospels begin with the words: "At that time Jesus…"? That doesn't refer to a certain time of the week. It refers to eternal time, a sacred moment, a time when God began to do something special, something to take notice of, something filled with meaning and purpose.

Now, what makes kairos or sacred time so special for Christians? What makes it special is the fact that it is not simply "one doggone thing after another." God time, kairos time, is filled with opportunities for salvation. It's a reservoir of grace. I guess we could say that chronological time or clock time is infused with kairos, with God-time, with sacred opportunities. In other words, for some people, time just keeps going around drearily from one moment to the next. They watch the clock so that they can go on to something more interesting. For the Christian, however, every moment of the day is pregnant with meaning, that is, if we are willing to look for that meaning and "capture the moment," as the ancient Romans used to say.

All this is summed up in Jesus' words in Mark's gospel for today: "Be constantly on watch, stay awake. You do not know when the appointed time will come." So, what is that "appointed time"? My sense is that the "appointed time" is not simply Sunday morning when we are celebrating the liturgy. The "appointed time" is at 7:00 a.m. when we get out of bed and thank God for another day. The "appointed time" is when we get to work or school and dedicate these hours ahead of us to God. The "appointed time" is the time during the day when someone unexpectedly asks us for help and we take the time to give it. The "appointed time" happens in the evening of the day when we are tired, but not so tired that we forget to tell God thanks for these eight hours of grace that have come flooding into our lives, drenching us with sacred experiences. All that is what kairos means—God in the day-time and God in the night-time, God in every tick of the clock, and every moment of the day. But, of course, as Jesus points out, it just doesn't happen automatically. We have to stay awake, and if we are awake and alert to the sound of God stirring in our life, there will surely be some wonderful surprises. A new year is upon us, my friends. Let us not miss out on what God may be planning for us. If nothing else, watch the clock, time is ticking away.

The Scriptures:
Isaiah 63:16-19 and 64:2-7;
1 Corinthians 1:3-9; Mark 13:33-37

Year C

Every so often, I read an article in the newspaper or hear something on television or radio about the danger that Big Brother is watching you. Actually, it's not a myth: Somebody, some Big Brother (maybe a Big Sister) is watching you. Ever since 9/11, as we all know, we have been living under heightened surveillance. In most big cities, if you happen to be walking down a main thoroughfare and if you choose to raise your eyes, you will see a little "not-so-hidden" camera peering down at you. Indeed, you may see several of these in a single block.

The reason for this surveillance, public authorities will tell you, is that they hope to avert incidences of violence before they happen or at least to find the perpetrators before they get away.

But despite all this caution, many people today are beginning to worry about the abuse of power, about the loss of private identity, or even about the possibility of being able to freely and innocently walk down the street without being watched over by some anonymous entity. It's obviously a different world since 9/11/01 and kind of scary. Who's watching whom these days?

But, again, authorities say: "Be vigilant. If you see something suspicious, report it." Unfortunately, however, sometime innocent people are reported for doing nothing illegal at all. At any rate, today the word is vigilance.

It may seem like a stretch, but for Christians who annually celebrate the season of Advent, you can expect to find all sorts of references to vigilance in the Scriptures for those Sundays. Don't become alarmed, however. This caution is not a reference to the electronic eye up there on the light pole. This warning to be vigilant comes from the early Christians' sense that the Lord Jesus would come back and come very soon as he had promised. Therefore, it seemed advisable "to be in the state of grace," as we once used to say, and not take any risks with our eternal salvation.

It's been some time now since that initial worry about Jesus' imminent return. Hence, we might ask, should we stop worrying? Well, I would put it in a more positive way. I think we should always be concerned about how we are living our Christian life, not with the worry that we might be "going to hell," but rather, we should be thinking about new and creative ways that we could live as Christians.

All this concern in the Scriptures about vigilance comes at the beginning of a new liturgical year, the new season of Advent, a very appropriate time to think again about the direction in which our Christian life has been going. So, with that, let me offer some suggestions about how to be vigilant as we enter the new liturgical year. The question: Are there any opportunities out there to live our Christian life in a more creative way? Or do we just continue on in the same fashion as we did during the last liturgical year? Here are some suggestions. They may not all fit everyone's tastes, but they may at least give you an insight you may not have thought of before.

First of all, Christian life is more than faithfully attending Mass each Sunday. Christian life is about "life," life lived in a whole lot of different ways. It's about learning and growing. It's about searching for new ways to experience Christ in our lives. It's about asking questions and finding answers. It's about dialoging with other Catholics to find out how they experience being Christian, even though they may not always agree with you about some issues.

So then, here are some thoughts on all this business of being vigilant:

Some day, get on the computer and check out the Vatican web site and see what Pope Benedict is saying. After all, he is our Catholic Teacher, the one responsible for orthodox Catholic teaching.

Or, you might want to check out the web site of your diocese to see what is happening in your diocese. There is just a whole raft of things on that site that could enlighten your faith.

Or, even closer to home, you might want to check out what is going on in your parish: Join a Bible discussion group. Sign up for a new ministry you have never tried before. Start a Catholic book club with your friends and read some good Catholic authors. There are lots of good ones.

Perhaps you may want to subscribe to a good Catholic newspaper or a magazine like *U.S. Catholic*. Or, if you cannot join a Catholic book club, check out the Catholic book section at Barnes and Noble. Or closer to home: Look up Google on your computer and type in "Things Catholic." Choose a topic and discuss it with your family.

Or, on the personal level, decide that every month during the coming liturgical year you will try to learn something new about your Catholic faith.

In short, all that I have been suggesting has to do with watching, being vigilant for ways to grow in your faith. Being

Catholic can be an exciting experience if we're vigilant and willing to look around for ways to go about it. No better time than now at the beginning of a new liturgical year.

Scriptures:
*Jeremiah 33:14-16; 1 Thessalonians 3:12–4:2;
Luke 21:25-28, 34-36*

2

Second Sunday of Advent

✝

YEAR A

WHEN I FIRST BEGAN THINKING about this homily back in October, the cottonwood trees across the parking lot from my office had completed their annual cycle of shedding their leaves. At this point in the season, with the onset of winter, one would never imagine that the sap under the bark of those trees was already preparing them to produce leaves next May. Experience tells me that this has regularly and predictably been happening every fall and every spring in the fifteen years I have been looking out that window. If I doubted nature's (and God's) power regarding that tree and nature's revival, my attitude about autumn and, indeed, life in general would be rather dismal.

Another metaphor of life and death comes to mind from Ken Burn's presentation on PBS of World War II with all its suffering and destruction. As I, a veteran of that war, watched the series, I thought to myself that even we who are old enough to remember those days have forgotten how terrible those times were, especially for the families who lost their loved ones. So, we can thank Ken Burns for the opportunity to be reminded of the suffering human beings can bring down on one another. Watching those films and still photos of the destruction of the cities of Europe and Japan, it occurred to me to wonder whether anyone in those times would ever have imagined that sometime in the future all these cities and villages would one day be rebuilt and that you would hardly imagine that a war had ever occurred there.

My point in both these examples is to say that given enough time and a sense of determination, the future of the world can always be restored. Human beings can bring life out of death.

If a person is to have any hope for the future, whether in one's secular or one's spiritual life, we need to have a sense of the long-term vision of life. Of course, that is often hard to do when at this moment in our personal or common history, life does not look very promising. Perhaps we are depressed with the continuing war in Iraq, or perhaps we are dealing with some personal problem that seems overwhelming. Unless we can think beyond this moment with its difficulties, however, to the possibility of a better time, life will not be very hopeful. In short, we need to think beyond this present moment if life is to have any meaning for us.

There are two Scripture readings in our liturgy for this Second Sunday of Advent, which can help us understand this sense of hope in difficult times. Life experiences in history do not change very much.

The first example comes from the prophet Isaiah. These were not good days for the Israelite nation. The Assyrians were in a conquering mood, and they were considered the most powerful nation in the Middle East in those days. They were gobbling up all the small nations around them much as Germany and Japan tried to do some fifty years ago. Israel, of course, was one of those small nations, and they were living in mortal fear of their future. Their leaders believed that there was no way for them to survive; hence, they had practically given up hope for their country and its people.

So, here is Isaiah, always the one who looked beyond the present moment, telling the leaders and the people that they need to believe that there is a future for them. He uses a metaphor like the example of the cottonwood tree I used earlier. He promises that in a future age, a shoot, a bud will spring forth from the land that considers itself almost dead. That bud or shoot will be personified in a man of wisdom, understanding, knowledge and strength. Historians believe Isaiah was referring to the young king, Hezekiah.

Christians, of course, have always interpreted Isaiah's prophecy to say that the one and only one who can ultimately bring peace to our world will be Jesus Christ. Notice the beautiful symbolic poetry of hope Isaiah uses: "The wolf will be guest of the lamb; the leopard will bed down with the young goat; the lion and the little calf will browse in the same pasture." In short, the impossible is possible if we hear the message of Jesus rightly. It may not happen today or right away, but it will happen.

Then we hear again, as we always do in Advent, the voice of a second Isaiah, John the Baptist, with his strange clothing, his odd eating habits and his fiery threats of destruction and what will happen unless the world changes its habits. Notice, John the Baptist chooses the tree metaphor again: "Every tree that does not bear good fruit will be cut down." The assumption, of course, is that there is life and hope under the bark of every tree, that is, in every human individual, every one of us, if only we care to make a difference, to make the world a place of peace and justice.

So, what sense does all this have for us, we who seem to live in a world where, like Isaiah's and John's, enemies are still enemies, where the wolf still threatens the Lamb? The only answer is that it does not have to be this way: Those of us who have been listening to Jesus' words all these years could be doing something to bring peace to the small world where we live and work. If being Christian means anything, it should mean that we, like the cottonwood tree I spoke of a moment ago, should recognize that we have in us the human and spiritual power to make a difference in this life, small as it may seem. The autumn trees, which may seem dead and dying now, have deep within them the power of spring. Perhaps, in the end, that is what Advent and this season of winter are saying to us. Spring will come and you can make it happen.

The Scriptures:
Isaiah 11:1-10; Romans 15:4-9; Matthew 3:1-12

Year B

These past weeks have surely been a harrowing time for our tender planet earth. It seemed almost as though nature was ganging up on its own world. First the hurricanes Katrina and Rita, then more recently the giant earthquake in India and Pakistan, then the rains and mudslides in Guatemala and finally more rain in the upper Northeast part of our own country. Thousands dead, many more injured, millions of dollars lost in destruction of homes and businesses. What more could happen? Many will obviously say: "It's all happened before. We will survive this one as we always have."

Of course, you also have the doom-sayers—preachers, radio commentators, and the talking heads—who claim that we are now living in the end times. For example, State Senator Hank Erwin of Alabama claimed on his radio program that "New Orleans and the Mississippi Gulf Coast have always been known for gambling, sin and wickedness. It is this sort of behavior that ultimately brings the judgment of God." A Methodist minister in his area responded by saying: "I don't know what sort of senator or politician Mr. Erwin is, but I can tell you one thing. He is surely no theologian!"

What the minister means is this. Any theologian with any sense would not claim that God punishes the world and its people indiscriminately by using earthquakes or hurricanes. Gambling may not be the highest calling in the world, but it surely does not invite the wrath of God. I'm sure that the good God-fearing mother and father in India whose home has been destroyed by the earthquake would find it hard to understand why God was personally punishing them. They are not gamblers, nor are they aware of any serious sin. We know that these sorts of judgments always happen, of course. Whenever there is some sort of natural catastrophe you will find someone who can find a religious reason for it. Beware of doom-sayers who can find God's hand in every tragedy.

I'm grateful that we do not have many Catholic preachers, theologians, or Catholics generally who believe in that kind of God.

The fact is that we have no idea, never have and never will have any idea about God's plan for this world, particularly its ending, if there is even to be an ending. We do know one thing, of course, and that is that Jesus said that he would come again, but whether that will coincide with the end of the world, we do not know.

We also know that Jesus said that "the kingdom of God is already among you,"—all of which means that God is working and has been working in this world in God's own mysterious way. The author of the Psalms puts it this way: "The heavens declare the glory of God and the sky proclaims its builder's craft." All this tells me that we can find God, if we want to make the effort, not in the destruction of life on the planet, but in its natural beauty.

So, here we are moving into the middle of Advent season which does, in fact, speak about endings and beginnings, not the end of the world, but of the many natural endings and beginnings that we see going on around us all the time. The point that Advent recalls for us is that God is in the middle of things, not in the end. So, it is in those events that we have a "theophany," a hint of Godness.

Time itself is constantly beginning and ending. We have calendars and clocks that try to help us keep track of time. An author I read some time ago put it this way: "Free us from being clock watchers, make us time lovers." What this means, I think, is that God is even to be found in that mysterious experience we call time, the space between events in our life.

How then does time begin and end? People who work with budgets can tell you. They know when the fiscal year begins and ends. (God in the numbers!)

Students know when the mid-semester and semester begins and ends and when term papers are due. (God in the grades!)

Politicians know when to start thinking about the next election (sometimes a year ahead of time, unfortunately for us).

Farmers watch the skies and know when to begin planting and when to begin harvesting.

Elderly folks know instinctively that their days are "numbered." If they are people of faith, of course, this is not a threat but a grace. All our days are "numbered."

For those of us who are Christian, we know that our Church year has natural beginnings and endings. It is good for us to know that life is not just "one doggone thing after another." When one season ends, we know that another will follow. In other words, there is a sense of hope in the Christian calendar because it is circular. It goes around and around. If we have missed opportunities for Christian living in the past, there will be more opportunities in the future. It's called the virtue of hope. God time is never ending time.

The question then comes to this: Not when will time end, but what are we doing in the midst of it to "redeem time." How do we use it well so that it does not go to waste?

The Jesus of Matthew's Gospel in the Twenty-fifth chapter gives us a pretty clear picture. We know that the Kingdom of God is getting close when we use at least some of our time to provide food for the hungry, drink for the thirsty, when we welcome the stranger, cover the naked and the homeless, visit those in prison. All those opportunities are happening right now in time, in our time, if we choose to make use of them.

So, I am not particularly concerned about the end of the world, even though there might be an earthquake or a hurricane somewhere in the world today or tomorrow. Those events tell me nothing. I do know this, however. There is still a lot to do in the world that I haven't gotten around to. I'm always behind time, as most of us are. So, let's stop worrying about end times and start thinking about what today's and tomorrow's opportunities will bring. Some exciting challenge may be just around the corner. Don't miss it.

The Scriptures:
Isaiah 40:1-5, 9-11; 2 Peter 3:8-14; Mark 1:1-8

Year C

I<small>F YOU WERE TO ASK</small> any Catholic person with even a smattering of catechism background in Roman liturgy what comes to mind when they hear the word Advent, without doubt they will say, "waiting" and "preparing." It is true. For all the years of our Catholic upbringing we have dwelt on those two words as the core of this beautiful season. Unfortunately, for many years, at least as children, we were told that we were waiting and preparing for the coming of Jesus or the birth of the baby Jesus—partly true, of course, but not true enough. There is so much more depth and meaning in those two words that we were not ready for in our early days. Are we ready for them today? That's the question! Here are some thoughts, not all original, but worth some reflection nonetheless.

I am sure it will be no breaking news to anyone that we humans spend a large portion of our life on earth simply waiting, waiting for something over which we have little or no control. It is probably one of the most frustrating feelings anyone can have, because by nature we are action-oriented; we want to do things, mentally or physically. However, we do wait nine months to be born. We expect that sometime in our eighties we will die. Then, in between those two parameters we continue to wait—to grow up, to finish school, to get a good job, to do a good job, to retire…and then what? More waiting. Some of the things we wait for in life do happen for us, others do not. Nonetheless, we have no other option than to wait.

In Raymond Brown's splendid work on John's gospel, he makes the point that even Jesus waited because he was convinced that the kingdom of God was close at hand. "You will know that the kingdom of God is coming close when the blind see, the lame walk and the poor have the good news preached to them." So, with that, Jesus, in some sense was struggling to hurry the onset of the kingdom of God. He wanted to do his part to make this event happen even in his own time. In his preaching, however, he continually made the point that waiting by itself is not enough. What is needed is vigilance, being on watch for God's coming, not necessarily at the "end times," but in the here and now.

In some sense, I believe Jesus is saying: "If the kingdom has not yet come, then we need to go about the business of making it come in our own day and time." The kingdom does not come spontaneously. Each age is responsible for the questions and challenges of their own time. In that sense, then, the kingdom is always coming but is not present yet. It's part of the old philosophical question of the already and the not yet. The kingdom is partly here, but not completely here.

Waiting around aimlessly, therefore, is not an option for the Christian. The kingdom comes every day. Indeed, Jesus says, it is already within you, already part of the ongoing action of this world. So, vigilance is the important point here, always being alert for whatever changes are going on. Time is important; events are always taking place in time. In themselves they have some meaning or the meaning that we put into them. In some mysterious manner, the kingdom comes at our pace to the degree that we are concerned about events that are happening in our age and time. Vigilance, vigilance is the central word. "Gird your loins" (put on your trousers), Jesus says. "Light your lamps," there is work to be done.

But then there is that other Advent word, "prepare." Prepare ye. You will notice that it is an active verb; do the hard work of preparing. Preparation events are happening around us every day. I'm sure there must be a large staff at the White House that prepares for the coming of important personages. Physicians prepare scrupulously for a surgery; lawyers spend long hours preparing their notes for a trial. Students spend years preparing for that final Ph.D. exam. Had we known how to prepare for the terrorist attacks on the World Trade Center, we might have prevented the deaths of over three thousand people. The person who is not vigilant, who does not know how to prepare even for the ordinary everyday events that take place in our daily lives, has some problems.

The question, however, is this: What sort of preparedness is called for in the season of Advent? Obviously, it is not the sort of short-term preparation that happens at the White House. Statesmen and women come and go each day. I believe that the preparation called for in Advent must come from the inside. It is the sort of attitude of mind or spirit demonstrated in the Scriptures in this Sunday's liturgy in the character of the prophet Baruch, of John the Baptist, and of Jesus. All their efforts were directed toward the events of their times. They saw issues that needed to be addressed and they addressed them. They also died for them. As for ourselves, living in this age of history as we do, Advent preparation must be for the eternal coming of the living word of God made flesh, Jesus Christ. This world in which we live is waiting for just such a word of good news—the cessation of war, attention to the poor, the diminishment of terror on our streets, et cetera.

Finally, it must be said that this Advent preparation and waiting would be all for naught if it were simply limited to Advent. What then happens to the rest of the year? Advent, in some sense, needs to be a model and a paradigm for the entire year, indeed for all of life. Christ continues to come with the invitation to follow Him where the blind still do not see, the handicapped do not yet have access, and where those without justice are still waiting. Human needs never seem to end, which means that our waiting and preparedness must never slacken until the Lord comes finally with the word that the kingdom is now.

The Scriptures:
Baruch 5:1-9; Philippians 1:4-6, 8-11; Luke 3:1-6

3

Third Sunday of Advent

YEAR A

BACK IN THE 1970s I SPENT three years in New York City doing graduate studies at Union Theological Seminary. Each day I needed to travel by subway from the Bronx, where I lived with the Holy Cross Brothers, downtown to 116th Street and Broadway in Manhattan, where Union Theological Seminary was located. Each morning as I ascended the stairs to street level I would notice a man with a long beard, a wool cap and heavy sweater, wearing a sandwich-board with the words: "The End Is Near." No one seemed to be paying much attention to him; he'd been there so long, I imagine. But occasionally I would say to myself: "What if he's right? What if the end is near? What then? Am I prepared?" Here I was, of course, going to the seminary to study theology with the assumption that if the end was near, it would probably not happen today. I imagine most other people entering or leaving the subway probably felt the same way, saying to themselves: "It's not going to happen today, so I might as well get on with whatever it is that I do in life." In other words, my hunch is that most ordinary folks do not believe that the end is near or even close.

It would be difficult even to get a consistent answer from people about what the end might mean. Does it mean the end of the planet? Does it mean that Jesus Christ will come again to straighten out the world? Nonetheless, I think if you asked most Christians and Catholics if they thought that this world and everything that people do in this world would last forever, they would tell you, "No, we are living, as it were, in the 'between times,' between now and the moment Christ will come again. That will be the final moment in history. What we are experiencing now is only temporary." Of course, if you asked a Christian, "Then what's next?" they probably would not have an answer. In short, what follows after life in this world is a great mystery.

It needs to be said, nonetheless, that Christians and other people of good faith have always struggled with the notion of end times. People generally do not believe that life in this world as we know it is the final answer to all questions, and yet we do not know how to believe in the coming of Christ at the end of time. How does one talk about that? The point is that our entire Christian life hinges on the assumption that Christ will come again and that Christian life in this world is only a preparation for God's eternal kingdom. We believe in all this, of course, but how do we talk about it? That is what our Scriptures for this Third Sunday of Advent help us to understand more clearly. How do we talk about mystery, about the unknown, about what we hope is or will be a reality someday?

We must grant, first of all, that the people of biblical times were as much puzzled about end times as we are today. Hence they chose to speak about them in metaphorical ways—first by poetry, and second by prophecy. Isaiah, whose words we hear in the first reading today, was a poet and prophet who lived in difficult times and tried to bring some hope to his homeland and its people. Hence, he used poetry to describe the mystery of God's coming. He says it will be like spring when the dry land will once again produce fruit and flowers. If God can bring life out of the dark and cold winter, so too can God continually bring life and hope to his people. Isaiah's poetry in that reading is just beautiful. It is the kind of writing that can give encouragement to any of us even today.

The gospel for this Advent Sunday talks about a man who resembled the man I mentioned earlier standing at the subway entrance at 116th Street and Broadway in New York City. John the Baptist believed sincerely that God had not abandoned the world and that someday God's plan for the universe would come to pass. But like the "prophet" with his sandwich-board in New York, he was convinced that this coming of God could not happen unless some preparation on our part would take place.

It occurs to me that what John is saying about being prepared for the final coming is what life could be for the Christian today. We have no idea what the future will bring, when the world will end, or when Christ will come again. So, we live, as it were, in "between times." But, that does not mean that we simply sit around and do nothing. Each time we gather for worship, as we are doing now, we are making Christ present and we are preparing for Christ's future coming. Each time we try to live our life as we think God has called us to do, we are making Christ present and preparing for Christ's final coming. So ultimately it does not make much difference whether or not we can predict the end times or when Christ will come again. It is the present moment that counts, and that is all-important. It is the only moment we have any control over anyway.

Perhaps the fact that I can still remember that man with his sandwich-board on 116th St. and Broadway in New York City warning me and others to be prepared for the end has helped me live my Christian life a little better. At least I'm not so anxious about when the end will come. It's already here. Actually, it always has been.

The Scriptures:
Isaiah 35:1-6, 10; James 5:7-10; Matthew 11:2-11

Year B

MOST OF US, AT LEAST THOSE of us who are adults, probably feel that we pretty much have control over our lives. We have a mind, we have will-power, we make decisions for or against things that pop up in our lives. That probably makes most of us feel pretty good. I guess, for the most part, most of us do have some control over our lives, or at least we would like to believe that we do.

But, just think for a minute about all the people who have control or at least some jurisdiction over you and your life. If you are a teenager, it's your parents. If you are a young adult in college, it's the professors. If you work for a living, as most of us do, you probably have a boss or at least an office manager who gives you orders or directions. Even those of us who are older often need someone to take care of us. Remember what Jesus said once to Peter: "Peter, when you were young, you used to go wherever you pleased and do what you liked. When you get old, someone else will bind you and tell you where to go" (paraphrase mine).

Then there are all the situations in the world we can't control and so we wait: Young couples can't wait for their first child. A mother waits patiently for nine months while the baby grows in her womb. Young people can't wait until they "grow up" and can leave home. Workers wait for a raise or a better job. Then, of course, there are always those annoying moments in daily life when we have nothing else to do except wait—the supermarket line, the light at the corner, the line at the bank, the appointment who is late.

At any rate, all of us are bound into systems of control. The police can tell us what to do; the courts can do the same. Even my bishop can tell me what to do, although he seldom does actually give me "orders." Even the Church or the Pope can tell us what to do and what not to do.

In short, if we are citizens and Christians, there will always be someone who will give us directions and even orders. It's the price we pay for being a citizen of this world. Perhaps it's even the price we pay for being human. We pay a price for growing up in life. It obviously doesn't happen all at once. Perhaps that is why we often find ourselves impatient with the pace of life. Nothing ever seems to happen quickly enough. Even this computer I am pounding away at never reacts as quickly as I would like. So, I wait, and wait.

It occurred to me once that waiting is actually part of world history. The world itself and life in the world move at their own pace and usually not quickly enough for us. Everything in the universe has been evolving slowly since the beginnings of creation and continues to do so from moment to moment. But in the meantime the world waits for our work to fill it up and to fulfill it with goodness.

I've often even wondered if God waits. I suppose you'd have to say that God has no other choice than to wait for each of us to "get our act together." Perhaps we could say that God has been waiting for all eternity for the world or the universe to become what God has planned for it. It's a great mystery. We'll never understand it.

I think it would also be true to say that Jesus had to wait around a lot. Obviously, he had to wait around for his apostles to catch up with his ideas about the kingdom. He was always asking them whether they still did not understand. We also know from Jesus' own words that he knew his own suffering and death were imminent, but could not do anything about that. So, he waited for the end to come.

Finally, I suppose we would have to say that Christ continues to wait for us and for his Church to become the Church which he hoped and planned it should become. The Church, of course, is us. The Church only becomes what we make it become. So, Christ waits.

All these thoughts come to mind as I reflected on the Scriptures for the Third Sunday of Advent. As Christians, we celebrate one season in the liturgical year which anticipates not so much Jesus' birth, because that has already happened long ago, but rather Christ's birth, the birth of the risen, resurrected Christ in the world every day. The word Advent itself means "a coming" or "a waiting for a coming."

So, what news do our two readings, one from Isaiah the prophet and the other from John the Baptist, have for us in

Third Sunday of Advent

Advent? The message I read there is that time is short. Time is always short, and life in this world is not a matter of simply waiting around for God to do things for us. Both Isaiah and John the Baptist tell us that while time is passing, while we are waiting, there are things to do. The world is waiting for us to "get our act together" and make God's kingdom come here and now. Isaiah said that the task for his time and for all time was to care for the poor, to heal the brokenhearted, to give hope to prisoners and to captives. In other words, to proclaim that there is hope in this world if we can find it in ourselves to care for those who are unable to care for themselves.

John the Baptist says basically the same thing. In fact, he actually quotes Isaiah: "I am a voice crying out in the desert. Straighten out the Lord's highway." In other words, John the Baptist is telling us that our task in this world, while we are waiting, is to discern God's will, not simply in our own regard, but how we fit into the lives of others, and how we try to bring about peace and justice, compassion and care for people who depend on us for those virtues. The point of all these words from Isaiah and John the Baptist is that the world we live in is still incomplete; it is always incomplete, always waiting for someone to make life more bearable, more just, more peaceful, more human.

All this does not simply happen in Advent season of course. Advent season is simply a short period in the liturgical year when we are reminded that time is always short, and there is still a lot to do to make the world a place where everyone is respected and treasured.

Finally, waiting may seem like a big fat boring time for many of us, something we can't do much about. But I always think of waiting like a room in a house that is completely empty, ready for us to fill it with furniture for life. So, the question comes to this: What are we doing while waiting? How are we filling up the spaces of our day with good works? If we can say that we have an answer to that, then there will never be another boring day. Every day we will be able to get up and say: "Well, Lord, what do you have in mind for me today?" And if we are willing to shut up and be quiet for a couple of minutes God will have an answer. I'd be willing to bet on it.

The Scriptures:
Isaiah 61:1-2, 10-11;
1 Thessalonians 5:16-24; John 1:6-8, 19-28

YEAR C

ALTHOUGH I KNOW LITTLE about classical music, I do appreciate some pieces that are well known by most folks. One such piece is Ludwig Von Beethoven's Symphony No. 9 in D minor, Opus 125, completed in 1824. It includes the music for a poem entitled "An die Freude" ("Ode to Joy") by Friedrich Schiller. To give you an example of Schiller's composition, here are some lines:

> Joy, joy moves the wheels
> In the universal time machine.
> Flowers it calls forth from their buds,
> Suns from the Firmament,
> Spheres it moves far out in Space,
> Where our telescopes cannot reach. (39-44)

Third Sunday of Advent

It might be worthwhile to read the entire piece while listening to Beethoven's music accompanying it. Beethoven's 9th has been used for church music and song for many years. We have all probably caught ourselves humming it occasionally. Even the European Union has chosen it as their official anthem. So, you can see how universally popular it is.

Given all this, my sense tells me that the music and words of the 9th Symphony might well be played and sung on this Third Sunday in Advent season, because all three scripture readings for this Sunday contain the theme of joy. Unfortunately, because of the length of the symphony, the liturgy might run a bit overtime—parking problems, you know.

At any rate, for those who remember the liturgy before the Second Vatican Council, the seasons of Lent and Advent were traditionally penitential in nature and theme. However, one Sunday, the third Sunday of both seasons, was always set aside as a "free" Sunday when the penitential spirit was lightened. Therefore, Lent's Third Sunday was named *Laetare* (rejoice) Sunday and the Third Sunday of Advent was named *Gaudete* (shout for joy) Sunday. Although the penitential spirit of Advent is not stressed so strictly today, the element of joy still persists.

The first reading for the Third Sunday of Advent comes from the prophet Zephaniah, who, like many of the other Jewish prophets, occasionally had hard things to say to the people of his country about their political and moral lives. "If life in the world seems out of whack," Zephaniah would say, "count it to the misdeeds of the people. Good morals, justice, honesty and compassion, on the other hand, will give the nation reason for rejoicing."

Then we come to Luke's gospel and the introduction of John the Baptist, never a very happy guy. He is constantly preaching doom and gloom to the people because of the quality of their lives. So, the folks listening to him rightly ask: "Hey, if you want us to do penance, just what is it that we should do?" Bad question, because they should already have known what they should do. So, John goes right on to tell them: "If you have too many clothes, give some away to the person who doesn't have enough. If you have enough for dinner today, make sure that your neighbor has some too. If you're a public official, don't use your office to line your own pockets. If you are in the military, don't get a big head over your rank. Your job is to protect your country, not to be a bully."

So, I think we can assume that if people are trying to practice the suggestions that John makes, there will be a sense of joy or at least satisfaction in the nation or the community. It probably does not always work so well, of course, but the ideal is good.

That brings up the question of joy itself—joy as we in the Twenty-first Century are used to thinking about it. We commonly think joy is like an interior sense of satisfaction or peace when all things are going well for us. We are filled with joy if some unsuspected piece of good luck comes our way. Or perhaps we are joyful simply if nothing catastrophic has happened today, and we can feel at peace. Or, finally, we may feel joyful if we have a sense that all is well in the world. All those are reasons for joy.

Of course, if we are honest about it, we have to admit that joy is not simply a feeling about something that affects us personally. I think our sense is that the world itself could be a better place, a more peaceful place, a more just place. That would surely bring a universal sense of joy to everyone.

Unfortunately it does not always happen that way. If that is the way we would like to think of joy, we will be sadly disappointed. Life in the world is not always going well. In fact, it is seldom going well. All we need to do is read our morning newspaper or watch "Good Morning America" or the "Today Show" to know what life is like in the real world on any one particular day. For example, on the day I write this many nations in the world are distressed over the fact (we think it's a fact) that North Korea has tested a nuclear weapon, and there is nothing even the United Nations can do about it. It makes the world a less safe place to live. No joy there! In the past several weeks in our own country there have been tragic murders of children in our schools: One episode in Bailey, Colorado, another in an Amish community in Lancaster County in Pennsylvania where five girls were killed and another five were seriously injured. No joy in those two communities, for sure. Moreover, there is surely no joy in the Darfur region of the Sudan in Africa where thousands are dying from rebel attacks or the lack of food and water, while the United Nations seems to stand by helplessly. Then, lastly, the wars continue in Afghanistan and Iraq where thousands of our soldiers and local civilians have died. No joy in any of those places either.

So, where can we find joy in the world? It happens in unsuspected places. Take the Amish community in Pennsylvania. Most of us could not believe their reaction when we read about it in the papers. On the day that Charles Carl Roberts, the man who shot the little girls, was buried in the local cemetery almost half of those who attended the funeral were members of the Amish community. Indeed, reports said that the community actually forgave Charles Roberts soon after the shooting itself. It is their way. They are Christian pacifists, and their rule is to forgive no matter what the circumstances. They take life seriously, and they forgave Mr. Roberts with honest intent. Radio commentators expressed amazement at this swift forgiveness, because this is not the custom among most Americans, even among Christians. We speak of forgiveness but do not always practice it despite our recitation of the Lord's Prayer each day.

So, reason for rejoicing does happen, not as often as we might like, but it does happen. The point is, we probably can't make it happen all over the world, but that's not our job. Our job as Christians is simply to bring some hope, some encouragement, and some joy into the small world in which we live and work. It is obvious that some people go out of their way to bring sadness into other peoples' lives. Given that, could there not be some way for us, for those who follow Christ, to balance life out, to do some little thing today that will give someone a reason to know that life is ok? Even a smile or a cheerful greeting will do it. It may not change the world, but someone's life will change and that's all that counts.

The Scriptures:
Zephaniah 3:14-18; Philippians 4:4-7; Luke 3:10-18

4
Fourth Sunday of Advent
†

YEAR A

SEVERAL TIMES EACH YEAR I have the pleasure and privilege of receiving birth announcements from young couples whose marriage I have celebrated. I can always tell that they are rightfully proud of their child, and it often becomes more clear in the name they have chosen, especially for their firstborn. Sometimes the names are not Christian names, of course, but they are always lovely and sweet. I'm sure the youngster will grow up, happy to be known by this unique name.

Undoubtedly, every Catholic has heard the story of the Irish monsignor who always insisted that any child he was asked to baptize needed to have a Christian name, at least for the books. Hence, if the couple had a name he did not particularly like, he would add Mary or John as a second name for the baptismal register! I'm sure the parents were a bit surprised when they asked for a copy of the child's baptismal certificate at the time of First Communion or Confirmation and found a name they did not even recognize.

I think it is true to say, however, that when parents choose a name for their child, they must ask themselves what their hopes are for this youngster. Will he or she bring honor and respect to the family? I know of couples that spend considerable time searching for a name that may have a special meaning. Other parents look up the history of the saint after whom they will name their child. They want to be able to tell this youngster all the famous things their patron was known for. All that, of course, can add much to the youngster's pride when people ask: "Hey, what does that name mean anyway?"

Birth announcements in Jewish culture were obviously made differently than we make them today. First, they were assumed to be made by an angel-messenger or by God in a dream; and, second, it was important that the name should have a meaning that would indicate the special role that this child would eventually have in the world.

Jesus' name, of course, came through the message of an angel. *Iesous* is a Greek rendering from the Hebrew *Yehoshua* (Joshua) which means, "to save" or the noun "salvation." That is why Jesus was later recognized as the Savior, the source of our salvation.

Most of us, I should imagine, simply live with the name we were given at birth or at our baptism without thinking much about it during our lifetime. Perhaps it is also true to say that we are not much concerned whether our name has any special meaning, Christian or secular. What does seem important, nonetheless, is to ask ourselves occasionally, perhaps often, what it means for us to be named Christian. Obviously, we could have been born into any other religious faith, but the fact is we are named Christian in memory of the Anointed One, Jesus the Christ.

Fourth Sunday of Advent

That should remind us to ask whether we have somehow fulfilled the meaning of that name as we have grown up in life. At age fifty, or sixty, or seventy-five, are we still proud to be called Christian or Catholic? Given that assumption, it might not be a bad idea occasionally to dig out that baptismal record, even if for no other reason than to discover who our godparents were or who the celebrant of the sacrament was. Perhaps all these good folks are now long deceased, but it must be said that they played an important part in our life at that moment in our history. Someone thought it important enough to bring us to a church and welcome us into the Body of Christ. That was the beginning of something important in our life, and the mystery of it all is that our Christening is still happening at this very moment. We are all Christians by name and Christian by calling until the Lord eventually calls us home.

The Scriptures:
Isaiah 7:10-14; Romans 1:1-7; Matthew 1:18-24

Year B

I AM SURE MOST OF YOU who have owned a home for a few years will tell me that your house, your home, is the most important thing that you own. The people down in New Orleans have been saying that over and over since Hurricane Katrina. In the floods they lost not only their house but everything in it, along with all the memories. We keep a lot of things in our homes that are precious to us. If we lose the building, we lose practically everything.

Homes or houses, as we all know, also house our own histories. I'm sure you have memories of the house in which you grew up. I would think that this house probably formed your psyche, how you look at life even today. It wasn't just the house, of course, but every event that ever happened there, good and bad. Houses form our very character.

Some years ago I had the occasion to go back home—well, almost home because the home where I grew up is not there any more. But it was important to me just to go back to the land where it once stood. I spent the better part of a day there just wandering around, letting memories flood back into my mind. I could even remember how certain events, some good and some not so good, have given me a sense of myself to this very day. Perhaps it was just as well that the house did not exist anymore, because it would probably have been in serious disrepair.

My point in all this is that the place where we were born, the place where our young consciences were formed, is important to us. Unless we have roots to go back to, we will forever be wanderers on this earth, lost without foundations.

Well, my friends, we come at last to the Fourth Sunday of Advent, and, as you might imagine, the Scriptures will be nudging us closer to the feast of the Nativity, which is only a week away. But surprisingly, the Scriptures for today are mostly about houses, houses for God, if you will, because the Feast of the Incarnation is fundamentally about the fact that God has come, and will come eternally, to make his home with us. Let us talk a little about houses—the houses we call temples, churches, chapels, synagogues, mosques. Fundamentally, they are rather odd structures—not odd architecturally or structurally, but odd in purpose. The question is this: Why should God need a house anyway? You probably noticed that theme very clearly in the first reading from the Second Book of Samuel. There is a little political conversation going on between King David and the prophet Nathan. David is checking in with Nathan, his political and religious adviser, to see if it would be ok with God to build a temple in Jerusalem. At first Nathan says, "Sure, go ahead." But then, after consulting with God, Nathan decides that this construction would not be such a good idea, because it was obvious to him that David did not want to build a temple to God, but rather to build a public edifice to honor himself and make himself look good and powerful among all the other kings of the Middle East who also had temples.

So, through Nathan, God says: "Look, for years I have not needed a house. I have been on the road, living in tents with my people ever since they came out of Egypt. Why do you now want to build me a temple?"

The point that God, through Nathan, wanted to make was that God truly lives among his people. That, in fact, is what the liturgy teaches us even today. God is with his people in the Eucharist, in the word proclaimed, in the minister of the Eucharist, but also in the hearts and minds of the people who have come to worship together.

The gospel backs the point of the first reading about God being eternally present with his people. Mary receives a message telling her that she will become the mother of God's Son, and that God Himself, through the power of the Holy Spirit, will make his home with her and with all of us for all eternity.

When you think about all this, it is really pretty astonishing. God decides to make his home in the human body of a virgin so that he can be with the rest of humankind forever.

You might say, what is so significant about that? Well, what is important is that if God has taken up his home in the womb of the Virgin Mary, this incarnation makes each of our bodies, each of us personally, a temple and a home for the Holy Spirit. That's a pretty astonishing realization, if you think about it a little. It should make us think of our bodies in a whole different way. Each of us is a sacred dwelling of God's Spirit.

I can remember some years ago, after celebrating the children's evening Mass of Christmas, standing near the Nativity scene and the crib, talking with folks. A little girl came up with her parents, and as she looked at the child Jesus in the crib she asked her mother: "Where does Jesus live for the rest of the year?" That may sound like a naive question, but it is also a question with some very profound implications, which only children could ask. If we don't know where Jesus Christ lives for the rest of the year, then Christmas ultimately does not make much sense.

The only answer I could have given to that little girl's question would have been something like this: "Well, true, Jesus is not in the crib for the whole year, but if you look around in church, you will see some people who come every Sunday to remember Jesus. That's the way Jesus chooses to stay with us all year long."

So, ultimately, I would have to say that God does not need a crib or a manger or a church, but God surely does need all of us. It will probably take a lifetime for us to get used to that mystery, but it's true nonetheless. Perhaps that's why it's all contained in the liturgy for the Fourth (and last) Sunday of Advent. We just need a little forewarning of the importance of the great feast we will celebrate next Sunday. It's almost too great a mystery to understand it completely just at Christmas.

So, when you go back to your home today, whether it is large or small, whether it is a house or an apartment, think of it as the place where you bring Jesus every time you walk in the door. So, we would surely have to say that we have taken up residence with God or that God has taken up residence with us. Either way, that's really not such a bad alternative when you think about it.

The Scriptures:
2 Samuel 7:1-5, 8-12, 14-16;
Romans 16:25-27; Luke 1:26-38

Year C

As I reflect on the past thirteen years when I have traveled to the towns and villages to celebrate the liturgy with all those Catholic people, I think of all the young folks I have "sort of" grown up with. I knew them when they were five years old, and now many of them are in college. Some of these youngsters lived in very small villages with small schools or no school at all. In such a case their parents did home-schooling. I remember in one instance a youngster who lived in a very small village that had no school. He needed to travel across a wild river by boat or air in summer and by snow machine in winter to attend school in another village. Despite the isolated location where he lived and the difficulty in getting to school, he was a brilliant student and ended up being accepted at Harvard University. By now, he may well be a CEO of some famous company. At any rate, coming from small places has no relationship to the quality of the folks who come from there.

I imagine many mothers and fathers must wonder when their children are born how they will make their way in the world when they grow up. Undoubtedly, they have high hopes. I am told that today parents often begin worrying when their child is in kindergarten whether he or she will eventually be accepted in an "Ivy League" college. No wonder high school students are under such stress trying to pass the SAT and to be in the top two percent of their class.

These thoughts came to me as I read the Scriptures for this Fourth Sunday of Advent with the references in the reading from the prophet Micah about a ruler for Israel that would come from the unsuspected little town of Bethlehem. It was predicted that he would be a shepherd-person and a man of peace. This Shepherd of Israel and Prince of Peace is indeed what the child born in Bethlehem did actually turn out to be.

I wonder whether Mary and Elizabeth talked about the future of their sons when they visited on that memorable occasion described in the gospel of Luke. Perhaps they were doubtful, like so many others, that anyone of any consequence ever came from Bethlehem. Yet, as we observe history, Bethlehem became the place that is celebrated today as the birthplace of the Savior, the Christ, the Good Shepherd—the one who would bring peace and justice to all nations. Again here is an example that the size of a birthplace has nothing to do with the future success of its citizens. I have a hunch that Jesus must have often thought about how people once looked down on the little village of Bethlehem where he was born. And the people who lived there must have been proud that the prediction of the prophet Micah came true for them and their village.

Like Jesus, most of us come from places that no one imagines are particularly important or will go down in history for producing famous people. But, again, like Jesus, our call is to go forth from this place where we were born and to follow our call to do things that will make the world a better place. It's all a great mystery—how we came to be born in this place and later find ourselves, like Jesus, following our vision in places we never imagined. Perhaps the lesson is that we must all at some time leave home to find out where we are meant to be, and what we were meant to do in life.

The Scriptures:
Micah 5:1-4; Hebrews 10:5-10; Luke 1:39-45

5

Christmas

✝

I'M SURE THERE IS NO DOUBT in anyone's mind that we would all like to be remembered for something during our life. How sad it would be if we were to come into this world and pass from it and no one were ever to take notice. Granted, few of us will be known and remembered for doing spectacular things. Nonetheless, the fact that we were here on this earth, the fact that we will leave some mark upon the human condition in the world should be noteworthy, at least to someone.

I have always thought that our birthday, the birthday of any human person, is probably the most important date in our lives. Obviously, there are other moments in our life that are equally important as well, but all these have to start somewhere, at some point in time. The day of our birth is obviously that moment.

Do you suppose that is why people generally celebrate birthdays with such joy and good humor? This was the beginning of something big, great plans, great hopes, even some disappointments, but it all started somewhere, at the point when we first appeared on the planet. That's the moment the human clock started ticking. So, one would think that this moment should be remembered and celebrated year after year until the moment we return back from this earth to the Father.

It has often occurred to me to wonder what Joseph and Mary must have been thinking about when Jesus was born. If he was, indeed, their first-born son as the gospels insist, it must have been a rather momentous occasion in their lives. I'm sure they probably asked themselves on a number of occasions: "What do you suppose this Son of ours will turn out to be? Will he ever be remembered for anything significant? Can we look at him and say that "we're proud of this Son of ours; he's destined for great things"?

It turns out, of course, that in the lives of each of us, we may have disappointed our parents. After all, we can't all be doctors, dentists, lawyers or politicians. Nonetheless, we all have found a place in life which probably satisfied us, and we need not look back in disappointment.

My hunch is that Jesus' mother and father probably had some second thoughts about the direction which his life took. The gospels actually tell us that at least his mother could not understand why he wanted to go out on his own to preach God's messianic kingdom. They thought he had lost his mind and wanted to take him home so he wouldn't be attacked by the "crazies" out there in the world. Nonetheless, Jesus kept to his vision, the call of his Father, until it took him to the hill called Calvary, where it all ended too early and too sadly.

But it all did begin at some point, at the moment of his birth, even though neither he nor his parents had any idea of where his life's vision would end. Of all the feasts of Christianity, Christmas surely seems to be the one that is most universally celebrated, even by folks who probably have little idea of why they are celebrating this day. I'm sure that the folks at all the Christmas "office parties" are thinking about other things when they break out the bottles and pass around the fancy hors d'oeuvres. Nonetheless, whether people in the world at large have any idea of the theological significance of this great feast or not, they know instinctively, I think, that this feast has some connection with Jesus' birth. Otherwise, why all the Christmas cards, the decoration of trees, the buying and sharing of gifts and all the rest? I'm sure most people are not concerned about the gross national product at Christmas. There is a sacred meaning in it for most people, whether they have ever read the Nativity story in Luke's gospel or not.

This may sound somewhat flippant to say about Christmas, but in the Christian liturgical calendar the Nativity is not the most important feast of the year. That honor goes to the Solemnity of Easter and also to Pentecost, the birthday of the church. But from the earliest days of our Church, the Nativity has held a place of honor, even though we do not know the actual date. For the early Church of Rome, it was simply a date picked to conflict with the secular Roman feast of the unconquered sun, the winter equinox. In other words, for the Christians, the birth of Jesus, the birth of the Son of God, light of the world, replaced the secular celebration of the sun. And so it has been ever since: We remember Jesus' birth, not simply as the birth of a human person, but the birth of the one who became known by all as the Light of the World.

So, even though Easter and Pentecost are important feasts for our Church, the only reason we can celebrate these great days is because, as the Hebrew Scriptures in the book of the prophet Isaiah proclaim: "A child is born to us, a son is given to us. They name him Wonder-Counselor, God-Hero, Prince of Peace." Had it not been for Jesus' birth in the flesh, there would be no reason to celebrate any of the other feasts in our Catholic calendar.

It would seem to me then that all of us here on this night (day) are here because in some mysterious way we know that something sacred happened in our world on the day that child we name Jesus came to birth. So we celebrate it in all sorts of ways, some secular, some sacred. We write greeting cards, decorate trees with lights, visit friends, celebrate good meals, and give gifts to one another. And we come here to celebrate the Eucharist together and to remember why all this is important to us. What we are doing here at this very moment invites us to turn our minds back to the day when it all started, when a young mother gave birth to a Son, whom the Church later called Son of God, Image of the Eternal Father.

So, whatever you may do on this night and this day, however you choose to celebrate this feast according to your habits and culture, it is a good and worthy thing you do. If it is important to each of us to be remembered for something on our birthday, so all the more is it worth celebrating the birthday of Jesus. That day was the beginning of something big, something the world is still celebrating to this very day because it is such a great mystery. I'm sure Joseph and Mary, from their place in heaven, are happy too that we still remember their Son's birth each year. At Christmas each of us can become little children again. Each of us can give gifts, because Jesus Christ is the greatest gift our world has ever received.

The Scriptures for Mass at Midnight:
Isaiah 9:1-6; Titus 2:11-14; Luke 2:1-14

6
The Holy Family
†

Year A

I happened to be chatting some weeks ago with a confrere at the Pastoral Center where I work, and we were reflecting on how it was when we were teenagers and how it was with regard to our parents. Not always so heavenly, we agreed. We were often pugnacious, belligerent, confrontational, truculent, and argumentative—all under the guise, so we thought, of finding our independence, although we would never have used that word. Now that we have grown in adulthood, we often look back on those days with shame and embarrassment. The fortunate point is, of course, that our parents were actually able to handle all this childish arrogance and move on to better things.

My friend and I also commented on the sometimes humorous situations where we must deal with our aged parents. How do you tell your father, for instance, that he might want to think about giving up his driver's license? The last two fender-benders did not bode well for his skills at the wheel! "Are you crazy?" he will say, "How do you imagine your mother and I plan to get to the market or to church on Sunday without a car? I'm as good a driver today as I was when I was in college." That is a moot question, of course, but the interesting feature about this conversation is that our fathers (or our mothers) are showing as much independence in this instance as we did when we were youngsters! Once you have lost your freedom, there's not much left!

The question is how does one speak to parents now that they are older? After all, they are still our parents. The answer is gently but firmly, as they once spoke to us. Logic does not enter the equation. Fraternal charity is the most reliable answer.

These thoughts came to mind as I perused the readings for the forthcoming feast of the Holy Family, particularly the words of Sirach, the wisdom-teacher: "My son, take care of your father when he is old; even if his mind fail, be considerate; kindness to a father will not be forgotten. Whoever honors his father atones for sins." No teacher today has said it any better.

From this follows the beautiful poetry of Paul in his Colossian letter—a passage I often suggest to bridal couples for their wedding: "Put on, as God's chosen ones, holy and beloved, heartfelt compassion, kindness, humility, gentleness and patience, bearing with one another and forgiving one another…and over all these put on love." No family counselor has ever said it any better.

The point in all this, of course, is that each of us progresses through periods of independence, whether as youngsters or people of age. We guard it with a certain fierceness. Having independence is part of our very human character; it's the way we come to know ourselves at the deepest level of our being. Unless we can test it occasionally, how should we come to know what are our limits or our gifts? I'm sure this must have been on Jesus' mind when he decided one day that he would hang out in the Temple where all people of religious importance hung out. Of course, he caused no little anxiety for his parents over it. Nothing further is mentioned in the gospels, so I presume it was all forgiven and forgotten.

I assume that all of us, when we reach a mature age, will want to reflect on the days of our youth occasionally and to hope that not too much harm was done by pushing the edges out a bit. No doubt, our parents would now appreciate the same consideration.

The Scriptures:
Sirach 3:2-7, 12-14;
Colossians 3:12-21; Luke 2:13-15, 19-23

Year B

ONE OF THE PLEASURABLE FEATURES of the Christmas season is the opportunity to learn what has been happening in the lives of the families that we love and write to, call upon, or deliver e-mail messages to each year. Some of the news is "so-so"—nothing much new this past year. Much of the news, of course, is happy news: "We have a new baby daughter" and "Our son graduated from college with honors." But tragedies are also told: "Grandpa died this year. Our son is in prison for smuggling drugs across the U.S. border from Mexico. Our daughter nearly died of an overdose, but she's okay now. Mom and dad separated this year. Economically, things are really tough here, and Dad has been out of work for several months."

You will recognize these as typical family stories, good and bad. They deserve to be told because they are part of our human condition. People look for understanding from their friends. When one member rejoices, all rejoice; when someone is experiencing sadness, all are sad. No matter what family we belong to, no one should ever need to rejoice or cry alone. In short, we are naturally glued to one another, and there is nothing we can do about it, fortunately.

Each year our Catholic calendar of feasts celebrates a special day to remember the Holy Family of Joseph, Mary, and Jesus, but it could just as well be the holy family of Bob and Mary, their son Jason or daughter Cindy, or whatever other family you might want to choose.

Such families may not wish to be called holy, but the very fact that they cling to one another, sometimes scold each other, weep with each other, defend each other, tells you immediately that this is, indeed, a holy family.

I am sure that Joseph, Mary and Jesus never imagined themselves a holy family, no holier than any other family in their neighborhood in Nazareth. Doubtless, they attended synagogue each Saturday morning and made a living as best they could.

Of course, their neighbors did not notice anything different about them either. This special recognition of Jesus as Messiah and savior only came later when he began his public life by preaching the kingdom of God.

I am convinced that families are holy by nature. According to the Book of Genesis, it all began when Adam and Eve recognized each other and, as the text states, "clung to each other." That is basically what every family in history has done; they cling to one another whether for good or ill.

In a sense, every family knows that if they do not cling to one another, support each other, no one is going to do it for them. There is a mysterious, inscrutable bonding among the members of the human race that seems to have its source in the very act of creation itself.

Of course, it is true that not all individuals choose to be part of the natural family, as we understand it—dad, mom and the kids. Some choose partners for life because of a natural but different sort of longing and attraction. Still others choose a religious family. There is something unique in this sort of larger bonding. Individuals choose it for the spiritual support it offers in prayer, meditation, and the ordinary activities of daily life. I can say from experience that this life is far from perfect, but we struggle and muddle our way through it joyfully. It is the only option we have. So, we are part of family of various sorts. If we did not have this option we would die of loneliness and despair. With no one to laugh with, no one to cry with, life can become nearly unbearable.

The story of Joseph, Mary and Jesus as we read it in one or another of the three versions we find in our Lectionary is a close match to the families I described above. Their lives were filled with the same joys, same sorrows, same tragedies that families in our own age experience: migration problems, poverty, and the power of the State and Temple always looking over their shoulders. Today we also have migration problems: people turned away from the border, raids on factories, husbands and wives and children separated from each other, terrorism destroying the fabric of family life, millions struggling to find food and shelter in Third World countries. Is anything so different than it was in the Holy Family's time?

So, what defense is left? To what security can this natural bonding of human beings look? It is a great puzzle in this age in which we live, where outside forces constantly threaten to break us apart. Nonetheless, it would seem that the natural instinct of clinging to each other, protecting each other, supporting each other, and even reprimanding each other with love can make life in this world not only bearable, but actually enjoyable. Did God create it all this way—this attraction, this bonding, this grouping and supporting? It surely seems so. Rabbi Abraham Joshua Heschel tells it this way: "Just to be is a blessing, just to live is holy." If there is any better option, I would surely like to hear of it.

Scriptures:
Genesis 15:1-6, 21:1-3;
Hebrews 11:8, 11-12, 17-19; Luke 2:22-40

Year C

It's an odd thing about our hard-nosed American society—in this modern age of communication, we hang on to every word of world news. Seemingly, we can't get enough of what's happening in Iraq, Afghanistan, Washington, Moscow, Beijing, London. Practically every public newsperson has a "take" on current conditions in the world. Bloggers are multiplying exponentially every week. I'm waiting for the Pope to open his own web-log. Of course, he already speaks from his balcony every Sunday at noon. He doesn't need a web-log.

What seems so common about world news, unfortunately,

is that much of it concerns competition, recrimination, war and violence: The daily "body-count" in Iraq, American soldiers and Iraqi civilians, and the nuclear build-up in Iran and North Korea suggest we are almost obsessed with wiping one another off the map.

Most of us would probably agree that family life in America has fallen on hard times. (It didn't seem so when I was growing up.) The attractions and distractions of secular society are not always conducive for families to learn how to live with one another helpfully and peacefully. It's tough being family today. Nonetheless, it seems to me that all of us have come to be in this world through the creativity of a father and a mother, and that we were nourished throughout our young life in communion with brothers and sisters. All that tells me that we are, as it were, "home made," created and brought up by those who cared about us enough to make sure we would eventually go out into the world proud of our heritage, thankful not simply for the genes passed on to us but everything human, including our religious faith—all that makes us to be this unique individual.

In other words, we are who we are through God's creative power, but we are also this person who goes by this name because of much care, nurturing, example, and even disciplining in our family. In other words, growing up takes a long time and demands a lot of care and feeding before we become the person God had in mind from all eternity.

One author I read put it this way: "The family is the place where we discover who we are and what we are capable of becoming. Family is the place where nature and nurture come together, the place where the members bestow on one another the lasting gifts that will be carried with us throughout our life."

On this feast of the Holy Family, therefore, I often wonder what it was like for Jesus to grow up in a family. There is a line in the gospel that gives us a clue: "Jesus, for his part, progressed steadily in wisdom and age and grace before God and men." Jesus grew up as we all do, and he probably had all the positive and negative experiences every young adult individual has. We also get some insight about Jesus' early life by noticing what he said and did as an adult. He was, for instance, a fierce defender of the poor and the oppressed, because he and his family had grown up poor and oppressed. The fact that Jesus had such a deep concern for justice and peace tells us what he learned at home. He didn't simply pick up those ideas on his own. He learned them from someone and they stuck with him throughout his entire life. In some sense then, all of us who are born into this world need some "finishing," some "polishing," some tender care in order to become what our heart and God's heart beckons us to become.

Finally, I have often wondered what Jesus looked like. Undoubtedly, he must have resembled his parentage. He must also have carried with him into adulthood all their human and emotional qualities. In other words, his family made him the one who he ultimately came to be. Perhaps it can also be said of us: We resemble our family; they have literally shaped and formed us the way we are. Who knows how we would have "turned out" without them?

The Scriptures:
1 Samuel 1:20-22, 24-28;
1 John 3:1-2, 21-24; Luke 2:41-52

7
Mary, the Mother of God

†

HAVING NEVER BEEN MARRIED, I am basically uneducated in the responsibilities of early child-care. I'm not complaining about that, of course, just making an observation. It has often occurred to me, however, that there must be a number of tasks that young married couples must attend to at the time of the birth of their first child. Learning about infant diets, sleep habits, what the sound of crying might mean, et cetera. After the first child, of course, all this becomes second nature.

The one responsibility every set of parents needs to think about, even before the birth of their child, is the name: How shall this child be named? I imagine there might occasionally be some controversy over that choice. It is no small matter, of course, because this name will stay with the child all the way into adulthood and beyond. So, it should be a thoughtful process.

The anomaly in all this is that the child has no part, no say, in this important lifetime selection. Indeed, the individual might well be disappointed and wished that he or she could have had their say, because they are the ones who have to "live with it."

I have often thought it might be best to give a child some sort of generic name at birth and then wait until the age of reason for a lifetime name to be chosen. By that time, obviously, the generic name will have been entrenched in everyone's mind and changing it might cause some long-term problems. I'm happy that I have never had to deal with this dilemma, if it is such.

I have never read any extensive commentaries by eminent scripture scholars on the gospel of Luke concerning the naming of Jesus. The text simply says "he was named Jesus." There is not much more one can say about that. But the name Jesus or Yeshua was a rather common name in those days. There was nothing particularly unique about it. It was as common as John is today.

However, if you read that text a bit more carefully, you will notice that Joseph and Mary actually had nothing at all to do with the choice of the name. The angel Gabriel had already given him that name even before "he was conceived in the womb." We must assume, therefore, that there must have been something prophetic about that choice. Indeed, the name Yeshua (Joshua) is simply translated as "Yahweh is salvation." Indeed, today we often hear the phrase "Jesus saves," and Christians believe that Jesus does save. Jesus is the source of our salvation. So, in hindsight, the name was well chosen whether Mary and Joseph had any hand in its choice or not.

So, after that little diversion, let us now make the point that this feast today is not simply about naming Jesus. This is the feast of Mary, who is the Mother of God. It is the oldest Marian feast in the Western Church. "Mother of God" was declared as an article of faith at the Council of Ephesus in the year 431 and placed into the Roman liturgical calendar for January the First sometime in the middle of the sixth century.

You might well ask then, why on January 1? Well, not simply because this is the first day of the new year but rather because we are in the Nativity cycle of the Roman calendar—the Christmas and Epiphany cycle. Hence, this feast fills out some of the history and implications of Jesus' birth. So, of all the Marian feasts, this is the oldest and the most meaningful for Christians. We honor Mary because she is the Mother of God, period.

Now, we must insist also that the naming ceremony is an important sub-plot on this feast of Mary. I'm sure you noticed in that beautiful selection from the Book of Numbers, the famous blessing that we use so often today: "The Lord bless you and keep you! The Lord let his face shine upon you, and be gracious to you! The Lord look kindly upon you and give you peace." I have given that blessing hundreds of times in my ministry as a priest. Let me insist, however, that it is not my blessing, or any priest's blessing. The blessing comes from the invocation of the name "Lord" or Yahweh. God or the name of God bestows the blessing. The priest just happens to be the instrument who calls down the blessing.

I would like to say then that there is something significant and important in this whole matter of bestowing God's blessing on one another. We all have that right, the right and power by our baptism to bestow blessings. Husbands and wives can bless one another. Parents should surely bless their children as they retire at night. Parents should bless their children when they make their way to school in the morning or when they go on a trip. In other words, all God's good gifts come to us through human hands, whether through the priest or, more often, through our bestowal on one another.

Lastly, think about this: God does not so much give blessings. God is a blessing for us. God's very existence blesses us. God's name blesses us. Jesus who is our salvation is also God's blessing on us. And finally think of this: As Christians, we ought to think of ourselves as God's blessing on one another, not so much by saying some words, but rather by the very way we live and the example we give of a good Christian life. That in itself cannot help but be a blessing.

So, let us go back to the question of naming our children. My personal feeling is that all of us should have a saint's name, someone who has a history of holiness and good deeds, someone whose history we could look up and try to imitate. In that case, a name would surely serve as a blessing for us for the rest of our lives.

The Scriptures:
Numbers 6:22-27; Galatians 4:4-7; Luke 2:16-21

8
The Epiphany of the Lord

†

LET ME TELL YOU a story about God. Actually, it is someone else's story about God, but it is worth retelling. Some years ago a reporter for the *New York Times* was sent to Guatemala to do a story on the civil war in that saddened country. He stood in the middle of the cathedral marketplace, where he observed people in a long line waiting for food. The line nearly extended around the block. At the end stood a slender young woman holding a basket. It seemed to take forever for her to reach the officials who were distributing the food. When she finally arrived, there was only a single banana left on the table. She looked off to the side where a little boy and girl were waiting by the fence. She then took the banana, walked over to them, peeled it, broke it in half and gave a piece to each of the children. They walked out of the square. At the end of the reporter's description of this event, he wrote: "You know, I think I saw the face of God just then."

Today we celebrate the solemnity of the Epiphany, my friends, the story of the three royal wise men who traveled across the Eastern desert to find and to pay homage to a child king, who was reported to have been born in Bethlehem of Judea. More about that later.

Many people throughout history have reported seeing the face of God or at least to having heard God speak to them. I have not been so fortunate. However, I can report that on many occasions I believe that I have experienced God up close. Was it an epiphany of sorts? I do believe so. An epiphany is simply an experience when the sacred, the awesome, the breathtaking overwhelms you and you can only say: "I saw the face of God just then."

Let me tell you of several such experiences that have left me without a human answer to life's epiphanies:

I think I saw the face of God early one morning when Father Jim Schultz and I took the last step on the summit of the Matterhorn in Switzerland and looked straight in the sun coming up over the border of Italy. An epiphany!

Sadly, I think I have seen the face of God in tragedy. On the day when I was called to a funeral home to take a crying mother by the arm to see her daughter, who had only hours before committed suicide, I saw the mysterious face of God just then.

I have watched little kids on a school playground screaming with pure joy for fifteen minutes of freedom. I saw the face of God

I have seen the face of God mysteriously, when I first learned that Father Jim Schultz, my friend and fellow-climber, had fallen off the east face of Little Bear Mountain in Colorado. He was dead; the mountains he so loved claimed him.

And finally, I think I have seen the face of God in those

earthy moments when a young man and woman say "I do"; or when a team of young, tight-muscled high school football players celebrate a win in the last five seconds of a game.

All these events, my friends, are epiphanies, visions of the sacred, whether in joy or tragedy. Each time a human being is so struck by the unexplainable that he or she can only gasp for breath and ask "why and how come," we are face to face with God.

I believe that is what the author of St. Matthew's gospel was trying to convey when he told that ancient story of the three royal personages from the East who came seeking someone who would tell them where the supposed King of the Jews was to be born. Why in Bethlehem—that small, insignificant, backwater village where nothing important in all of history has ever occurred? Now that's the face of God and the work of God.

And so, as the story goes, these royal princes came to visit the God-king and pay their homage: gold, frankincense and myrrh. What astonished these men, of course, was the fact that the light of a star was constantly directing them to the place where a child lay—yes, astonishingly, a child and a king.

Somewhere in that story there must be a message for us, who so often imagine that we live in a dull world where nothing spectacular, nothing dazzling, nothing brilliant ever happens. Could it be that we have closed up our eyes to the light of the spectacular, the overwhelming and the events that draw from us a simple response: "Holy smoke, how about that"?

I truly believe that there are holy events, unexplainable human experiences happening at nearly every moment of the day and just waiting for a person of imagination and insight to say: "You know, I think I saw the face of God just then." By the way, we do not even need to brave the miles of hot desert sands to experience the sacred. It's all around us, free for the imagining.

The Scriptures:
Isaiah 60:1-6; Ephesians 3:2-3, 5-6; Matthew 2:1-12

9
Baptism of the Lord

†

YEAR A

AS THE NEW YEAR BEGAN its slow and toilsome course through history, accompanied by much noise and celebration, it occurred to me that the beginnings of many formal events in our personal and national history also seem to require a certain attention and celebration. But as with many well-planned formal events, the threat of chaos also lurks in the wings.

Observe, for instance, the high-church attention we pay to presidential inaugurations, which occasionally end in a rather indecorous and embarrassing manner. Point of fact—one presidential inaugural candidate insisted on riding down Pennsylvania Avenue on his favorite horse in a cold rain. Six weeks later he died of pneumonia. In another instance, a president's wife died of pneumonia after having dutifully sat through her husband's inaugural speech that lasted over an hour. During the inaugural speech of President John F. Kennedy, a small electric heater beneath the speaker's podium caught fire and almost demolished the entire platform. If I remember correctly, the beloved and dignified poet, Robert

Frost, experienced some difficulty in delivering his poem at the same inaugural event.

Despite such setbacks in formality, of course, we will go to great lengths to call attention to these important historical-political moments. The same might be said, of course, of certain significant moments in each of our lives. The newly appointed CEO of a company receives special acclaim with a formal party. Novices in religious communities make formal vows when they are prepared to commit themselves permanently to this life. As a sign of their acceptance into religious life, a crucifix is given them to wear and generally a grand soiree follows. Priests are ordained in a well-planned formal ceremony as a sign that they will henceforth have the responsibility of caring for God's people and a grand banquet ordinarily follows. The names of judges and doctors often appear in the news when they accept their responsibility in medicine or law. The point of all this is to say that the beginning of any career deserves special notice and acclaim.

So, what about Jesus? Did he ever experience anything in his life that could even remotely be described as an inauguration ceremony? It might not sound particularly important, but I would like to suggest that there was a moment in Jesus' young life that convinced him that he (like any national leader) was called to do hard and challenging things. It happened one day at a water ceremony in which he personally chose to take part. In the midst of this public bathing, which he received at the hands of John the Baptist (himself something of a radical), he heard a mysterious voice calling him a special Son and inviting him to do God's hard work of proclamation, healing, justice and peacemaking. I interpret that event as an inaugural moment in Jesus' life, the instant when he discovered his vocation to literally change the world. We know what came of all this, of course. He went directly out into the desert to think about the implications of that experience in the river. When he returned, he immediately went to work talking about a new kind of kingdom that described what the world would look like if God had a hand in it.

All of that prompts me to ask the question whether any of us have ever experienced a similar "inaugural" calling. Most of us were too young to notice any special voice naming us at our baptism. However, the call was there, and the best way to discern its meaning today is to check out the date and circumstances on our baptismal record. That's when it all started. The end is not yet in sight.

The Scriptures:
Isaiah 42:1-4, 6-7; Acts 10:34-38; Matthew 3:13-17

Year B

If I had to do it over again, I think I might have asked my parents to delay my baptism until my 18th birthday (or somewhere around the age when adulthood blossoms). Obviously, I had no say in that. My parents, like most parents, lost no time (two days after my birth, as a matter of record) in having me baptized, because they wanted to have the assurance that if my fragile little life were suddenly to end as quickly as it had begun, they and I would at least know that heaven awaited me. "No Limbo for this kid," they probably said to themselves. I can't say that I blame them. What parent would want to consign their loving child to the murky confines of that theological construction called Limbo when they could as easily be comforted in the thought that baptism would carry me straight to God's kingdom? So, it was done without delay and without my consultation! Just as well.

Nonetheless, I cannot imagine a compassionate and loving God who would not shed a tear over the death of the least of his creatures, and who would consign this little human child to an unknown future simply because his parents were not able to get to the church in timely fashion for his or her baptism. Can God's love possibly be constrained by the accidents of human life or the lack of parental foresight? It would not seem so to me! No doubt, baptism into Christ is tremendously important for every human person, but not as a means of forestalling the implications of a sudden and unsuspected death with an unpredictable eternity. Indeed, Limbo is no longer a Church teaching.

The gospel for this feast of Jesus' baptism relates a privileged event in his life, one over which most of us have no control. Jesus chose to be baptized as a mature, fully-grown adult. He had already been circumcised as a child, of course, but that was a ceremony with a different meaning and purpose entirely. The baptism of Jesus is a rather odd event, when one thinks about it. In simplest terms, the gospels tell us that one day, almost purely by accident, Jesus happened to be in the neighborhood where John was baptizing in the Jordan River. Not knowing, perhaps, what was involved, but not wanting to be left out of this public penitential ritual either, he presented himself to John for the great washing, which seemingly went off without incident. However, as the gospel of Matthew points out, when Jesus came up out of the water, he had this astonishing experience of the Spirit coming down upon him and hearing a voice tell him: "You are my beloved Son, with you I am well pleased." In short, this penitential washing ceremony presented itself as the opportunity for Jesus to begin his adult public life. Until that moment, Jesus was a respectable, unexceptional, and unnoticed woodworker in a backwater village called Nazareth. Apparently, there was nothing in his previous life that prepared him for this decision to go on a mission that had no sanction from the Temple officials. His mission was purely his own decision to start a way of life and a career that in many ways shocked and offended his mother and his neighbors. From the moment he came up out of the water, he was a man-possessed, possessed by the Spirit to go into the world and change it forever, which, in fact, he did. Family life, the carpentry trade, the quiet life in Nazareth was obviously not for him. His vision was broader and deeper than that.

My hunch is that Jesus probably began to think about his future long before meeting with John at the Jordan, but that day presented him with the opportunity to make publicly a break that he was waiting for and to set out on his grand venture. This encounter was to be the watershed day in his life, the moment from which he could not turn back. In short, it was not so much what the baptism ceremony did for Jesus, but rather what he did as a result of taking part in it. In other words, vocations have to start somewhere, and this baptism is where Jesus started.

All this still leaves us with this question, however. What does or what should our baptism mean in the context of our own life and future? Obviously, most of us were baptized as infants. When does our vocation begin? I would have to say that the spark, the Spirit, the call is instilled in us by God at our baptism, but it quietly hovers or smolders there until we can begin to see or understand what direction our life should be taking. Of course, that may change or develop many times during our lifetime with each decision building on the former one. Most of life's decisions do not happen once for all. The opportunities occur again and again. They depend upon age, maturity, and opportunities which we notice along the way—options which we take advantage of. In other words, vocation is an on-going experience continuing to happen during our entire life.

So I have a hunch that even Jesus began to think about his vocation long before he was baptized. He probably saw all sorts of things happening in the world of his time that he wanted to do something about. The baptism day was simply the moment when he publicly decided to "go for it."

So, does it ultimately matter whether we are baptized as infants or as adults? I would say that if we understand baptism as God's on-going call to us, it makes no difference at all. What is of more importance is that we use our opportunity here and now, this once-and-for-all encounter that is offered to us at whatever age and do exactly what Jesus did. Accept the call and the challenge to go about our work in the world as though this were the most important thing that ever happened to us.

Do you suppose that Jesus began to think about his future when he was a teenager in the woodshop sanding down doors and window frames? I'd be willing to bet that he did some dreaming, and that he probably said to himself: "Someday I'm going to take the opportunity to leave this town and this place and do great things." Little did he know that the day he accidentally wandered down to the Jordan River and joined that crowd would be the very chance he was looking for. We know what happened after that, of course. The rest of his short life was set in stone.

Now, the question is this. How many opportunities have passed us by to do great things for God and the world? Hard to say, of course, but if baptism gets us ready for the rest of our life, chances are there will be lots more. It's just a matter of recognizing the right time and the right place, like Jesus did. Of course, like Jesus, we have to accept the fact that there is no turning back. Vocations, at whatever point they happen in our lives, are forever.

The Scriptures:
Isaiah 55:1-11; 1 John 5:1-9; Mark 1:7-11

Year C

I have known only a few people in my lifetime of whom I could say that they truly chose to live outside the human community. Mind you, they were not lonely people; they simply chose to live within their own psyche and their own chosen world. At the same time, it does not seem to be the "normal" pattern of life. Most of us, as the author of Genesis insists, cling to one another out of fear, fear that we shall become isolated and lost in that universe out there that seems not to have place for us. You make it on your own in life or you don't make it. "Loneliness and the fear of being unwanted is the most terrible poverty."

It is obvious to most of us, of course, that we choose communities of people who love us, support us, defend us, laugh and cry with us. Fundamentally, we are made for one another. That is why we seek out communities to our liking. If they will have us, we are saved. If they shun us, we will go elsewhere until we find true companionship. It is fundamentally about our very salvation. Having said all that, let us speak of the loneliness of Jesus.

On this Sunday we celebrate an event critical to his life, his baptism—an event of mystery for many Christians. So, why did Jesus join the crowds that day at the Jordan River and take his turn in the water? Obviously, it had nothing to do with sin, original or personal. I would rather believe that he, like many of his fellow-Jews, believed in the power of water to cleanse, physically, of course, but spiritually as well. My sense, then, is that Jesus wished to declare himself as one, like all others, who felt the human need for repentance. The washing simply fulfilled his deepest desire to identify with his brothers and sisters, who after all were part of his race and history. This tendency to be part of his own people remains consistent throughout his entire adult life and ministry. He identifies with a group of Seventy-Two, with the Twelve, indeed also with special friends, such as Lazarus, Martha, Mary, the Pharisees, and the social outcasts and people of the street. The gospels seem to describe Jesus as a person desperately searching for companionship.

Perhaps the most poignant scene in his life happens

when Jesus needed someone to stay with him during his last hours. "Could you, my friends, not stay awake with me even for an hour as I face my final trial?" The need for personal companionship to the very end seems obvious. I am sure that I must speak for many of you when I say that there have been moments in my life when I was ready to abandon this ministry. Had it not been for a few dedicated friends who refused to let me take that path, I may well not be writing this.

I have this sense that, deep in the psyche of each of us, lies the desire to be needed, to be of personal value to someone or to many, to find respect among others, to be known as this human individual whose unique identity will never again be replicated in all of history. We create our own happiness just as we create our own loneliness. People are lonely because they build walls instead of bridges. Walls block our dreams; bridges link us to that future we so deeply and naturally long for. It's that simple.

The Scriptures:
Isaiah 40:1-5, 9-11;
Titus 2:11-14, 3:4-7; Luke 3:15-16, 21-22

10

†

First Sunday of Lent

YEAR A

SPEAKING OUT OF MY OWN EXPERIENCE and perhaps assuming yours as well, I would be willing to say that most of our "Lents" have been disappointing—not necessarily a disaster but perhaps less than satisfactory.

As I began thinking about this homily for the First Sunday of Lent once again, I asked myself the question: "Why does Lent turn out so badly for me? Why have I consistently been dissatisfied with my 'performance' during these forty holy days of penance and self perception?" Well, I think I have just answered the question. Perhaps, without knowing it and without planning it so, it's been a "performance." I don't necessarily mean a stage performance, but rather some grand plan that will change my life forever. That would be my heart's desire, I said. But, my friends, it's never happened. I've never really changed my life radically, at least not in the limited time of forty days and forty nights.

I'm sure you have all made so-called "good resolutions" at the beginning of the year or at some other significant moment in your life's history. But how many of those resolutions have we kept and been satisfied with? Not many, I'll wager! So, what's the answer? Is there an answer to this annual question of ours: "What are we going to do for Lent?" That's the way the question is often phrased—"doing something for Lent." If what we planned to do for Lent was actually so important, why wouldn't we want to be doing the same throughout the entire year? Perhaps there is a hidden thought that if we do something for Lent, it may stick for the rest of the year. At least that may be the hidden hope whether we express it that way or not. Alas, it does not always happen that way.

I have decided, however, that this year I may take a different approach to Lent. The idea came to me from the title of a smallish book I'm reading by Jim Martin, the Jesuit who writes for *America Magazine*. It's entitled: *Being Who You Are*. The title sort of fascinated me because the tendency for us usually is to be different than we presently are. So, what I'm proposing for myself this year (maybe even next year) is to promise less and to think more, to simply reflect more on who I am at this point in my life, to get a clearer sense of my personhood and how I think of myself. Perhaps from all this some truth will be forthcoming. If all that means fewer penances, less discipline, so be it.

The reason I think this may be more effective is because the incentive comes right out of the Scriptures assigned for this Sunday. The first reading comes from that lovely story of the creation of Adam and Eve, their temptation and their eventual fall from grace. Scripture scholars have been reminding us for years that this is not a story of a lush garden, a snake and a piece of fruit. It's not a story about who was ultimately responsible for succumbing to the snake. It's really a lot deeper than all that. It's really about the state of the human condition, of how we got to be the way we are. It's the story of Everyman and Everywoman. It's ultimately a story also about how we humans deal with choices. In both Genesis and the Gospel you will notice that the main characters, Adam and Eve, and Jesus, are faced with choices that will ultimately make them more human or which will detract from their human nature.

So, there are a lot of ultimate questions in the Genesis story. For instance: Why are we like we are? Why do we do evil? Why is there suffering? Why do we often feel alienated from God? Why do we often make wrong decisions when we obviously know better? Why are we ashamed of our actions? Good questions all. But whoever that author of Genesis was, one thing for sure, he was not afraid to look human nature in the face, and he didn't like what he saw. He knew that it was not just the first Man and Woman who made bad choices. Bad choices are being made all the time, and that is obviously the reason for our shame, alienation, guilt and the daily struggle to get out of the mess we're in. Could that ultimately be the reason why we feel that it is important to "do penances"?

Finally we come to that well-known story of the three great temptations Jesus experienced. Those are all about choices too, just like the one in Genesis. Matthew, the gospel writer, frames those battle temptations as though they were going on between Jesus and another person, who is the evil spirit. But, actually the battle is going on in the mind of Jesus. How will he deal with easy answers to life's questions? Each one deals with a different human option, all attractive, rewarding, and fulfilling—at least on the surface. Besides that, they won't cost anything. But notice, in each case Jesus thinks it through and refuses to be fooled. He knew that he was stronger than all the temptations combined. And he said no!

So, here we are back to the question of knowing and being who we are and dealing with life's questions from that vantage point. I'm actually grateful that Lent gives us the opportunity to think about all that and if we do we'll ultimately be the better for it. Is it still a good idea to do penance, prayer, fasting and almsgiving in Lent? Absolutely! But not to demonstrate how tough we are but rather to discover the real person that we are, and how we deal with those choices that will go on long after Lent is over.

The Scriptures:
Genesis 2:7-9, 3:1-7;
Romans 5:12-19; Matthew 4:1-11

Year B

THE CHRISTMAS SEASON is complete now, and with that we know that the next season will be Lent and Easter. In some sense I think that we are never quite ready for Ash Wednesday or the First Sunday of this season. On the other hand, we welcome these six weeks because many issues in our life have probably been building up over the past year and we know in our heart that we need to confront them.

Lent, truly, is a gift for us all. It is a different kind of season, a serious time, a time of reflection and new intent. Would we really get serious and take a broad look at our life if the Church did not offer us this special time? Speaking for myself, probably not. For that reason then we need this special push, this engagement with the reality of our lives. I always look forward to Ash Wednesday and those weeks that follow it, because I know that I will come away the better for it. Yes, it's true, we will all come back to revisit Lent again next year and the year after that, not simply because of liturgical law or a sense of guilt, but because deep down we know that time and the world are hard on us. Indeed, our own weak spirit does not help us much either. And so given all that, we feel happy that we have the whole Church supporting us in this huge effort to turn away from sin and follow the gospel once again.

As the old saying has it, on Ash Wednesday and during Lent sin goes to Church. We go to Church because we know that we are not alone in this huge effort of renewal and reconciliation. We will be in Church, among the community of the faithful giving our all to this great effort of discovering who we are and where we belong.

The question, of course, that arises at Lent's beginning is, "So, what am I going to do this year?" From past experience we know that the options are overwhelming. We will go to church daily; we will read some special spiritual book we have been putting off, and, of course, following the suggestion of the Scriptures, we will pray, fast and give alms. I have no argument with any of those ideas, except to ask the question: "Why?" Why are we planning to do all these things? In some sense, I suppose, we have the hope that these will change our life, or we will choose to do them for penance sake and to make up for our wrongs. Nonetheless, from my own experience, I can tell you that penances are not magic. They do not solve or eliminate long-entrenched habits. But, still and all, we continue the practices because we feel so good afterward. We've made the great effort, and that in itself seems to be a reward.

For my part, however, I am always brought back to the Gospel on Lent's first Sunday, the one you just heard—Jesus being driven by the spirit into the wilderness where he faced the three universal temptations that we all experience in our own lives. Here is what happens: Jesus has just recently been baptized in the Jordan by John. Then immediately he goes out into the desert, the quiet places where there will be no distraction, and there he will think about his life now and about his future. Will he go the way of other young men of his time and make a name for himself? Or will he listen to that quiet voice deep within and try to figure out what this mysterious call means?

We all know the answer, of course. His choice is still making us wonder today, wonder what the Good News means, what the Kingdom of God means, and what justice and peace and concern for the poor means. It was to these issues that Jesus eventually dedicated himself.

All this leads me to say that all the so-called Lenten practices we have "practiced" before are not in vain, but rather that they must be preceded in doing what Jesus did—think and reflect and ponder about who we are just now and what we are capable of for God's kingdom. In other words, Lent, it seems to me is first of all a time for deep interior reflection. Who am I just now? What gives my life meaning, what is my bliss and what continues to keep me from achieving that Christian goal I set for myself each Lent? Obviously, if we are thinking about

Lenten penances, this one will surely prove the most difficult of all because we usually will insist that everything is really okay in our life and promising to do a few penances will make it all perfect.

My own suggestion, therefore, is simply to keep quiet during Lent. Do some good spiritual reading to deepen our sense of self. Spend at least fifteen minutes of reflection daily in our own desert. I am not sure whether there will be any noticeable external changes in our life by Holy Thursday, but at least we will have had to face ourselves and ask hard questions. Chances are that we will not notice many spectacular long-term changes in our life-behavior, but that's not the goal. The goal is simply to take a serious look at life as it appears to us just now and let the spirit move us in the right direction.

The Scriptures:
Genesis 9:8-15; 1 Peter 3:18-22; Mark 1:12-15

Year C

I HAVE A FEELING THAT the person who was responsible (I'm assuming it was a Pope) for the good ordering of the liturgical calendar, the ordered procession of Sundays and feast days, obviously did not take the condition of human nature into consideration. It may sound trivial, but it has only been approximately six weeks since we celebrated (yes celebrated) the Nativity of the Lord and the other lesser feasts that follow directly after it. And now, here we are today on the First Sunday of Lent being asked to put on ashes and dreary faces (well, not quite). However, we are asked to change our thoughts to serious matters. I'm not sure whether most Christians are ready for that substantial transformation. Whether we are prepared for it or not, however, the season has come for us to do some serious thinking about the manner in which we look at life and what we are doing about it.

Of course, the anomaly in all this is that Lent is not for the sake of Lent. Lent is for life and living. Lent is a time for rethinking the patterns of our life to see whether they are leading us anywhere beyond the season itself.

Traditionally, we Christians have always opened the Gospel for this Sunday with the description of Jesus' three temptations, and how he dealt with them. The graphic language of the gospel has Jesus fighting against outside worldly forces: satisfaction with self (stones to bread), power and glory (world domination), casting himself off the highest point of the temple (power over self).

The "old time" Lenten preachers would collapse these three into a familiar saying: "the world, the flesh and the devil." Using the graphic description of the three temptations in the gospel, they assumed that human temptation came from the outside. Seriously minded people, they thought, were constantly harassed by powers beyond their control.

A more serious reflection on this passage, however, gives one the sense that any person, any human being, any Christian is fundamentally faced with self and with those inner urges that rise out of one's psyche when in contact with the world. Remember the old Pogo line: "We have met the enemy and he is us." The gospel story seems to say that the world and its allurements have the power of evil, in a sense that, unless controlled, they will destroy a person. Jesus is portrayed, of course, as the one who has faced these temptations and overcome them, and this example is a model for the Christian as well. Admittedly, of course, the world around us does have an effect upon our life, but only if we allow it to do so. We are all children in this world, but hopefully not of it. I want to insist that it is not the world that is out to conquer us. It is our inner desire to react to those natural inner forces that rise up against us. Who of us has not felt the power to control our environment? Who has not lusted after the world's attractions? It is not the world or its goods that are to be blamed; it is the uncontrolled inquisitiveness arising out of our emotions that causes us anxiety.

In this regard, Sister Joan Chittister, a Benedictine nun in Erie Pennsylvania, has an interesting insight on the relationship between the world and the self: "In the midst of chaos," she says, "it is nevertheless possible to be at peace, because peace first comes from within ourselves, not from outside of us. Those who are not at peace within, would not be at peace in heaven." Given what Joan Chittister says regarding peace, we might well think of it as the predominant goal for Lent. Lent is not about overcoming "the evil one," nor about conquering our inner tendencies. Rather it is about coming to grips with self and making peace with ourselves. Ultimately, life for the Christian is not about battling the world, imaginary or real. Rather it is about understanding the world as friend, brother or sister. We do not necessarily need to be "at war" with what attracts us.

With all that in mind, I am convinced that when the forty

days and forty nights of Lent are completed and Easter dawns, we will be at rest and at peace with ourselves. Have a peaceful Lent, my friends.

The Scriptures:
Deuteronomy 26:4-10;
Romans 10:8-13; Luke 4:1-13

11

Second Sunday of Lent

†

YEAR A

IT HAS ALWAYS BEEN a great mystery to me why it is that I can clearly remember certain events in my life, some going all the way back into my childhood, which were not very significant in themselves. And yet, others that should have been very important to me, I have no recollection of at all.

As a child, for instance, I can remember my father playing the violin (fiddle!) in the living room of our home, and my being spellbound by it. Playing the violin in one's home must not seem all that important, and yet I remember it clearly to this very day. Or again, I can still remember the first airplane I ever saw up close. I can even remember the name of the pilot etched on the side of the plane.

However, I cannot remember the celebration of my First Communion, my Confirmation, or even parts of my Ordination ceremony. You would think that these solemn religious rites should have made an impression on me, and yet, alas, they have disappeared from memory. The human mind is a great mystery. Why does it retain some human experiences and forget others? Without doubt some events in our human history have made an indelible impact on our consciousness, for whatever reason.

I think the same might be said of certain events that have taken place in our country's history or even in the history of the world. Fortunately, there were individuals who remembered them and had the good sense to write them down for the sake of history. Everyone of age, I'm sure, remembers Pearl Harbor. Similarly, everyone remembers "9/11" and everyone remembers the names of the cities of Hiroshima and Nagasaki destroyed by the atom bomb. Interestingly, these events are not religious in nature, and yet many people interpret them spiritually, because they had such a negative impact on the human race. They might even be interpreted as death and resurrection experiences for humanity. At any rate, they will not be forgotten by previous generations or by generations to come. We could almost call them transcendent events transcending time and place. Our Scriptures for this Second Sunday of Lent contain two such transcendent experiences that have never been forgotten. The first comes from the history of the Hebrews. It is remembered as the call of Abraham, the Father of the Israelites. Interestingly, it is referred to three different times in the Book of Genesis, which will tell you that it had a definite impact on the consciousness of the Hebrew people. Three different scribes wrote it down. The reason it was important to the Israelites was that, for the first time in human history, we have a record of a people being given a piece of land of their own and a place in history. All this gifting was done by God according to the Hebrew interpretation of the event. I'm sure there is not a Jewish person in the world today (whether practicing or not) for whom this is not an important moment in their history. It defines who they are.

The gospel also has a remembrance story. In this instance, however, only three people remember the event—Peter, James and John, the disciples of Jesus. Let it be said, however, that it is mainly a remembrance story in the life of Jesus. It happens on the top of a mountain, which tells you immediately that it is meant to be interpreted as a story of transcendence, a sacred moment in the lives of Jesus and the disciples.

We are not completely clear how this event happened because some of the references are metaphorical, such as the cloud and the voice speaking out of the cloud. Nonetheless, Jesus is clearly speaking to God the Father, and this intimacy is a complete mystery to the three disciples. They don't understand it, but they know something important and something sacred is happening. Hence, they feel they must build some sort of stone remembrance—a cairn or a rock pile for history. They also carried the event in their memories until another generation could write it down and we could also experience it today. So, what are we to make of all this? Several things come to mind. First of all, most human events that happen to us are holy. Rabbi Abraham Heschel once said: "Just to be is a blessing. Just to live is holy." If that is the case, it would be worthwhile for us to try and remember as best we can those events in our lives that were sacred to us, whether religious or not. Perhaps they could even be written down for another generation.

Think, for instance of Thomas Merton, the Trappist monk who wrote the story of his life entitled *The Seven Storey Mountain*. Think too of St. Augustine's autobiography, *The Confes-*

sions. Both of those life accounts have influenced the lives of many, many people over the years. So, perhaps our story is also important. Some say that we live on our memories; we forget the bad ones and try to remember the good ones. It is all part of our history and all worth remembering.

The Scriptures:
Genesis 12:1-4; 2 Timothy 1:8-10; Matthew 17:1-9

Year B

"Thou shalt not kill." Four words, the Fifth Commandment of the Decalogue, God's own Word. You can't get it much clearer than that! No killing, period! But isn't it interesting that in the history of the human race we have probably had more violations of that commandment than any of the other nine.

I suppose we would not have needed God to tell us that killing is wrong. It is obviously part of the natural law. None of us would want our life taken from us; so what should give us the right to take someone else's life, for whatever reason? Of all things that are precious to us, life stands in first place. Perhaps that is why we Americans in particular have been struggling with the death penalty or capital punishment for so many years, indeed, until this very day. What bothers many is that we have found that in too many instances innocent people have been put to death. One innocent death is already one too many. I must confess to you that I believe that the death penalty is unjust. Granted, murders of innocent people are a horrible and unjust act. However, I always wonder if one death deserves another. Moreover, does capital punishment actually deter violent crime? I have no evidence one way or the other on that. Moreover, most violent crimes which take life occur because of anger, vengeance or retaliation. That is no excuse, of course, and punishment of some sort should follow—life in prison at the least.

This important question always follows: Does capital punishment harden our sense of compassion and forgiveness? Well, this is a depressing way to start a homily, even on the Second Sunday of Lent, but we cannot pass up the question, because our first reading from the Book of Genesis contains that famous and very puzzling story of God's command to Abraham to offer up his son Isaac in sacrifice. I have read all sorts of explanations for that atrocious act. God didn't really mean it; he was just testing Abraham. Or, the fact that God relented is a proof that God forbids the human sacrifice of children, an act that many cultures had practiced for centuries.

Consider the stories in *National Geographic* that describe the sacrifice of little children in the high places of Peru. My own understanding of those primitive cultures is that the life of a child was the most precious thing they possessed. The very future of the family or clan depended upon the life of this youngster. Hence, if they wished to please their god, the life of a child would surely suffice, horrible as that may sound. For centuries the human race has felt the need to appease god(s) with their most precious gifts.

In our own times, of course, some theological questions arise about God and sacrifice: If God wants sacrifice, wouldn't grain or animals do? Why would a good and just God, who brings all human flesh into existence, suddenly want us to sacrifice the most precious being on earth—a human being? Moreover, why should God want to test us anyway? If God gave us a human mind and will, could God not simply trust us? Or, finally, does God expect human sacrifice at all, or is it just a desire on the part of humanity to appease God?

Well, fortunately, in our own time, child sacrifice is history. Were we not all shocked when the lady in Houston some years ago drowned her five children because she thought God was calling on her to do so? We all knew that she must have been mentally ill. But let us be honest about this issue as well. The lives of children are being taken every day in our country and in our world. Abortion may be legal, but it is, nonetheless, a horrible taking of life. What is equally heinous today is the crime of pornography wherein little children are made the subjects of sexual fantasies. Why are little children made to suffer this inhuman form of recreation? More and more today we also learn from news accounts of the numbers of children who are battered by their parents and sometimes killed. Why take advantage of a defenseless little child? As Catholics, we cannot pass over the fact that priests have taken advantage of their position and sexually abused youngsters in their teens or younger. Again, why are young people the ones who are abused by adults? Is it because they seem more vulnerable, or that they will not speak out in their own defense? The point I am making is that we may well read in horror the biblical story of Abraham's willingness to take the life of his son Isaac, while at the same time we think little of the taking of life in the womb or the abuse of children and teenagers by adults that goes on day after day in our own time.

So, what has all this to do with Lent? Lent, obviously, means a lot of different things to different people, and we all have our little projects to fill up the Forty Days. It may be something as small as abstention from chocolate or whatever our other little "evil spirits" are. On a more positive note, we may wish to get serious again about the age-old practices of prayer, fasting and almsgiving. Stations of the Cross or Lenten Vespers put us in liturgical touch with others. But whatever practice we may choose, these are not ends in themselves. They are meant to help us understand transformation—turning around again. That, indeed, is what Lent is about. The Greeks call it *metanoia*, a turning completely around again. Doubtless, this will not be a final turning around, given our human inclination to be slackers. But if we care to link Lent to that first reading about the sacrifice of little Isaac, we might well think about transforming our attitude toward the preciousness of life in all its various and beautiful forms. Transformation is always a matter of the head and the heart. Given that we are always a little slow and sluggish about changing our ways of thinking and doing, perhaps the Forty Days will hardly be enough, but they will be a start which may carry us all the way into the days of summer at the least.

The Scriptures:
Genesis 22:1-2, 9-13, 15-18;
Romans 8:31-34; Mark 9:2-10

Year C

It has often occurred to me that most of us are naturally destined to be contemplatives, that is, searchers for silence. That may sound like a rather odd suggestion, because the fact is that all of us live in another world—the world of work, of recreation, of noise and responsibilities which makes contemplation, if not impossible, at least rather difficult to find. Nonetheless, if you were to ask the ordinary blue-collar or white-collar person if they would prefer to have some opportunity for silence in an ordinary day, I'm certain they would say, "Sure." Of course, we live in a world of noise and distraction simply because we must. There is no other option if we want to make a living. But paradise, according to Genesis, was never like the world we live in today.

I have often thought to myself that if I had not been born and raised a Catholic and if I did not have so many years invested in the Catholic Church, I might think about joining the Quakers or the Amish. Alas, it's too late at my age. Nonetheless, I long for some quiet every day. It's available to me, but I seldom make use of it the way I should. The question is where to find it.

I have told this story before, but when I was a youngster, living on a farm, the land around us was predominantly flat, but near our house there was also a rather impressive hill. No mountain, mind you, just a bump on the plains. But it was one of my favorite places to go when I wanted to be alone. Sometimes I would go there and watch for my father coming home from the fields in the evening. But mostly, I would go there because it was quiet. I could see for miles, I could feel the sun and the wind on my face. It just seemed good to be there.

Actually, I was not old enough to imagine that I was in touch with God on that hill, but if someone asked me why I spent so much time up there, I would probably have said: "It's just quiet, that's all." Actually, I have always been fascinated with hills and mountains. Later in life I enjoyed many experiences climbing truly big mountains. That same feeling of peace always overwhelmed me when I reached the top.

I have often had the sense that Jesus must have been torn between a life of contemplation and action. We all know from the gospels how much time he literally spent among the crowds, healing and preaching. But once in a while, when it became too oppressive for him, he would say to his friends: "Let's get away from here and go to a quiet place where we can pray."

That seems to be what happened on a day Jesus invited Peter, James and John to accompany him to a high place to pray. Notice, the text specifically says that Jesus wanted to pray on a high and quiet place. He wanted to literally be in touch with God. So, it is described as a transcendent experience, a divine experience. The symbols are all there—the cloud that envelops them, the meeting with Moses and Elijah, the voice out of the cloud designating Jesus as God's chosen one. The interesting point is that we do not know whether Jesus and his friends actually prayed or prayed as we usually pray. They just experienced God. Even Jesus' disciples seemed to know that this was something special that they should preserve for posterity. Therefore, they suggested to Jesus that it might be a good idea to set up three altars in remembrance of the occasion so that they could return again some day and pray.

I imagine most of us would not choose to climb a mountain to pray, but if we had the option, I imagine we would choose some quiet place where we would be undisturbed and be with our God. Perhaps we could say that each of us already has a place of that sort where we pray—our parish church, a grotto somewhere, a local convent or monastery. The point is this. We all long for a prayer place and we will take time off occasionally to go to it.

Why are we hearing this gospel of the Transfiguration on this Second Sunday of Lent? Here is my suggestion: Lent is a special time of self-discovery, a desert-space experience, a time when we are invited to make a special effort to find ourselves and re-find our direction in life. Every season of the year, of course, is "prayer-time," but Lent is a special time, a desert time or a mountain time when we might want to learn how to pray more sincerely and to be in touch with our God.

Contrary to the way we have traditionally thought about Lent as being a "give up something" time, I would suggest that it could be much simpler. If we did nothing more than make the effort just to be quiet so that God could make God's way into our life, that would be enough for Lent. If nothing else, we should be able to come out of this Lent being able to say that we have been looking for a place where we could be thinking about God. I doubt whether we would be ready to say that we came away transfigured like Jesus was, but that's not the point. The point is that God will meet us in some way and somehow wherever we try to set aside some place and time for

Him. It doesn't necessarily have to happen on a mountain, or even on a modest hill, unless you think you are actually ready for some strenuous exercise, which, by the way might not be such a bad idea either.

The Scriptures:
Genesis 15:5-12, 17-18;
Philippians 3:17–4:1; Luke 9:28-36

12

Third Sunday of Lent

†

Year A

MY HUNCH IS THAT MOST of us don't often think much about being thirsty. The fact is that we are probably never very thirsty. Oh, yes, I suppose we'd all love to have a coke or a beer on a hot day. That would slake our thirst at least for a little while. But none of us, I suspect, has ever been so thirsty that our lips began to crack or that our tongue and throat were so dry we could hardly speak. That sort of thirst doesn't happen today, at least not in First-World countries. But it does happen in many parts of the world, especially in the desert areas of Africa or the Middle East.

Even in the United States today wars are being fought over who gets the water from the Colorado River. Should it go into the swimming pools of Los Angeles or the vegetable growers in the Central Valley of California? Even the state of Georgia is worrying today about the water level of the lake that supplies Atlanta's homes and businesses. There is no doubt that water is in the news and the minds of many people today, more than it ever has been before. Even "Global Warming" is causing people to worry about oceanic water levels. But for the moment let us say that we don't immediately need to worry about going thirsty today or tomorrow. The question, however, is this: Do we experience a thirst for anything else in life? I'm talking about thirst in the analogical sense, a longing or a craving for other things besides water, something that could give us a reason for living. I'm thinking, for instance, of our thirst or our longing for love, for recognition, for support, for respect, for intimacy, for partnership, for community, for peace, for identity, for meaningful work, and especially for the sacred and for God. We are all very complicated people. There are lots of things we long for even though we have more than enough water to drink.

An added thought about our thirsting is this: Do we ever give a thought to the notion that we have it in our power to slake the thirsts of others, that each of us has a hidden well that we can draw on and make it possible for others to live? Obviously, none of us has the capability of fully taking care of ourselves. We naturally depend on each other to lighten our thirsts for whatever it is we long for. The point is that we don't always know where the well is, but someone else does, so we go to that person to draw the water for us.

There are two examples of that in our Scriptures for this Third Sunday of Lent. The first comes from the Book of Exodus, the migration story of the Israelites through a land where there was little water. There were occasional springs (oases) along the route, but you had to know where they were. The immigrant Israelites were getting desperate. They were ready to give Moses the boot and go back to Egypt. Fortunately, just in the nick of time, Moses finds a spring and saves the day, along with his life. So, we are back to the question: Who knows where the water is? Is that person ready to make the water available to those who are thirsty? Remember, you can't hoard water. It's too precious.

The second story comes out of Jesus' life. He was obviously on the road a lot. He needed to know where the "watering holes" were. Fortunately, there was a famous one. Everyone in the Middle East knew where Jacob's well was. So, here we have Jesus and his twelve followers (all men) out of water and even without a bucket, and coming to Jacob's well. Fortunately, a woman from the nearby village is already filling her jar. Whether they liked it or not, Jesus and twelve men needed to ask a woman for water! That may have been considered humiliation for men in those times, but what could they do? She had the bucket and the water! No questions asked.

But then Jesus and the woman get into this very interesting theological conversation about the water of life and the question of where one can satisfy one's thirst for God. So, there is an interesting trade-off. Jesus and the guys get a drink of cold water, and the woman receives from Jesus some insight about how to slake her thirst for God—a "win-win" situation all around.

All this brings us back once again to the question: "Who's thirsty and who has the bucket and the water, so we can we make a trade and everyone will come away satisfied?" That's the question for the modern Christian: Who's thirsty and who's got the water?

Finally, why are we hearing all this on the Third Sunday of Lent? We are hearing of water, because in practically every church in Christendom some folks are thirsting for acceptance into the Catholic Church. They are in an RCIA program, and they are only a few weeks away from the "well"—the fountain of baptism. These two stories therefore are catechism lessons for the catechumens. They are the thirsty travelers and the Church is the "well" that will satisfy them at the Easter vigil. My hunch is that all of us who have already had our initial thirst for God satisfied at baptism should now be ready to share the water of our faith with others. So, again, we're left with the question: "Who's thirsty, who's got the bucket and the water, and is there anyone willing to share?"

The Scriptures:
Exodus 17:3-7;
Romans 5:1-2, 5-8; John 4:5-42

Year B

I AM SURE THAT THERE ARE MANY experiences or memories from our past that we could say have given us a sense of identity, a sense that we belong somewhere, that we have something that gives us reason for existence. The first of these, I should think, would be our home, especially the house where we lived and grew up in our early years. There must have been a sense of stability that we enjoyed in that place. Perhaps there were even special rooms that we could call our own, where we could be alone to think and play.

I have a memory of such a house. It was a large Victorian-style house, with lots of rooms. Being the only child in the family for a number of my early years, I could claim the whole place for myself. It was my personal castle where I could pretend I was king or at least a prince, and everyone else was my subject. Later on, of course, I had to share it with other brothers and sisters, but I can still remember every nook and cranny of that place. I don't think I have ever lived in any other house that has had the same impact on my life. I still hold a vivid image of it in my mind.

Why should that be so important for me? Well, I think it has something to do with a sense of place, a sense that we belong somewhere specific, a place where there is warmth and protection, an assurance that we are safe there. I'm sure most of us would raise our voices in protest if someone decided to take it from us. We might even think of that home as a sort of sacred space where we prayed with our parents and where we first learned our catechism, et cetera.

The second building that we may remember from our youth and that may have left an imprint on us might be our church. We always say that churches are "ours" because in a sense we know we can go there whenever we like and that we will be welcomed, if not by an "usher," then surely by the God whom we were told dwelt there in the tabernacle with the lighted red candle-lamp burning nearby. It was quiet there; there was a sense of awe and holiness when you came in. It may even have had the smell of incense and of the crowds of people that packed the church each Sunday. Churches do seem to have a unique odor of holiness!

It is again interesting that we could call this church our very own. It was the Irish church or the German or the Lithuanian church. Other folks had their churches and we had ours. We might not even have felt comfortable in one of those other churches. This church is the place where family events took place: Baptisms, First Communions, Confirmations, weddings and funerals. We could expect that our spiritual needs would be satisfied there.

So, theologically, why are churches so precious to us? Well, I think it is because we have the deep sense that here is where we meet our God. Here is where God takes up residence with us when we come. No other building can compare with this one; it has a specialness we call sacred. That is why we give churches special names, names of the saints or one of the mysteries of Christ. Here is where our Christian character is formed. It is also a place that we would defend against all harm.

It would not be out of place, therefore, to say that Jesus also had his favorite "church," a place where his character was formed by the teachings and rites that were held there. It was the great Temple that King Herod constructed over many years. Parts of it still remain standing today. People come to pray at the so-called "Western Wall" every day.

So, we learn in the gospel for this Third Sunday in Lent how Jesus felt about this Temple, where he had learned something about God when he was but twelve years old. By the time he was about thirty, of course, he had felt a special call from God to preach good news, to heal the sick, and to raise the dead. But he also had the need to pray at the Temple occasionally, to experience the quiet of the sanctuary, perhaps to make an offering. It was this need for quiet time with his God that drew him to the Temple on a particular day. Perhaps he had not been there for a while. At any rate, when he walked in he found that commercial enterprises were being transacted there, at least in the outer courts. Now, we do not have much evidence that Jesus got really angry during his life, but this is one instance that stands out very clearly. Jesus seemed genuinely shocked at the sight of the selling of animals and birds for sacrifice, and at the money that was changing hands. When you read the details of the event you say to yourself: "Jesus really lost it; he became violent." It must truly have been a ferocious scene, tables flying, money scattered across the pavement, birds and animals running wildly about, people yelling. It would have made a good subject for a film, and it actually has been done.

The odd thing about all this is that most of the other people who came to the Temple to pray seemingly did not get agitated by all the commercialism going on there. This tells me that Jesus had a deeper sense of the sacredness of the Temple than many others of his day, and he was willing to go to extremes to defend its sacred character. We also know from reading further in the gospels that this event got Jesus into a heap of trouble with the Temple authorities as well as with civil leaders. The conflict led eventually to his passion and death.

So, what does all this have to do with our sense of Church today? Obviously, we do not have ushers sitting in the entry way, making change or charging "pew rent"! Tickets for parish functions are sold outside or in the hospitality rooms of the church, or wherever. But churches today are places that serve a variety of human needs and hospitality surely. Churches are also places where we should have the freedom to meet God on our terms. Aside from the common liturgy, we should be able to drink in the meaning of the symbols that surround us. We should be able to come away from this time with God refreshed, quieted and satisfied spiritually. There should be no distraction. At the same time, we should feel free to take part in the sacred liturgy with passion and delight along with our fellow-Christians, because we come there as a community and not as individuals. In a sense, churches are places where there is room for everyone's devotion and everyone's spirituality. We need to make room for each other. In short, if "homes are places where, if you go there, they have to take you in," so are churches.

The Scriptures:
Exodus 20:1-17;
1 Corinthians 1:22-25; John 2:13-25

Year C

I RECENTLY FINISHED READING a fascinating book by Timothy Egan entitled *The Worst Hard Time*. It is the actual history of the great drought that left the high plains of Texas, Oklahoma, Kansas, and Colorado a vast dust bowl in the middle-thirties of the last century. I happened to hear it reviewed on National Public Radio one morning and decided to buy it right away, mainly because I too can clearly remember the dust bowl days in my native North Dakota. The book is actually about six families who decided to "stick it out" on the land during those terrible years, in contrast to the people who are described in the novel *The Grapes of Wrath* as the ones who left the land and headed for California.

The book is a story of people, but even more, it is also a book about the land—the earth—specifically about the vast millions of acres of grassland across four states over which the Indians had roamed for thousands of years pursuing the buffalo and the antelope. At the turn of the century, the U.S. government opened up this vast pasturage to farming, and immediately thousands of "hard up" farmers descended upon it, plowing up earth never meant for farming. At the outset all looked good. People raised wheat and looked forward to a life of millionaires. But then came the hard years of the "thirties" with the lack of rain and the high winds that literally picked up the earth of the plains and sent it wheeling as far east as New York and Washington, D.C.

Herbert Hoover lost the presidency over that catastrophe. Franklin Roosevelt was able to set in motion some reclamation programs. Nonetheless, the Great Plains have never fully recovered. Whole towns have disappeared, never to be repopulated again.

I just wanted to talk a little about all that, because it has to do with the sacredness of the earth—the land on which we live. In this case, the land was thoughtlessly desecrated, ripped up, torn up and so it simply blew away—a great act of disrespect upon the natural world. I am sure that most of us do not often think much about the earth as "sacred," as holy. It is simply something natural, something from which we make a living. We think of the "bread basket" of the Dakotas or the vegetable and fruit basket of central California as being ours to do with what we choose. We think of "Global Warming" as a modern myth which won't affect our generation. It has always seemed to me, however, that anything that gives life is inherently holy. Anything God has given us to sustain the life of the planet must somehow be sacred.

The people of the Middle East have always had a special respect for the earth, perhaps because they live so close to it and depend on it for their existence. The great patriarchs, Abraham, Isaac and Jacob, eventually settled the "Promised Land," because that is where there was water and one could grow things and live.

We have a beautiful story in today's first reading from the Book of Exodus about the sacredness of the earth. It is the familiar tale of Moses, the nomadic shepherd out in the desert, who notices a dry bush strangely burning. He decides to "check it out," but immediately he is warned not to come any closer, but to take off his sandals because he is standing on holy ground. I have never been able to figure out why wearing shoes should desecrate the earth. If you are shoeless, perhaps you are in closer touch with the natural elements. Just a guess! When Moses does come closer to the burning bush, however, God begins to speak with him and reveals His name as "I AM." The implication I draw from this experience is that God does speak out of the earth, if we have the good sense to consider the earth as God's domain.

I think people have always found the experience of being close to the land a transcendental experience. Why have monasteries of monks and nuns always been established far from cities in forested land or simply out in the country? Why do people find comfort and spiritual renewal by going out into the wilderness to make a retreat or simply to be in closer touch with God? Even people who simply like to "grub" around in their garden find it a peaceful and comforting experience.

So, what does all this have to do with Lent? Well, Lent has traditionally been a time when we, like Moses, are invited to come in closer touch with our God again. It may not be possible for most of us who live in this cold, wintry environment to go out and get in touch with our God in the soil of the earth, but perhaps we could create a virtual piece of earth for ourselves where we can be quiet and in touch with ourselves. Whatever works! At any rate, God often speaks to us in strange places—no burning bushes, perhaps, but in whatever place is already holy for us. If we go there, God will surely be ready to have a word with us.

The Scriptures:
Exodus 3:1-8, 13-15;
1 Corinthians 10:1-6, 10-12; Luke 13:1-9

13

Fourth Sunday of Lent

†

YEAR A

SEVERAL WEEKS AGO my optometrist suggested that my eyesight was becoming a little cloudy, and that it might be a good idea for me to have cataract surgery. At first it sounded pretty threatening. I didn't want anyone messing with my eyes, unless it was absolutely necessary. I've had these eyes for a lot of years, and they have served me well. But Dr. G assured me that it was not dangerous, that the operation would take only a short while, and I would definitely see more clearly afterward. And so it was. I'm seeing things today that I never saw before! Flat-screen television never looked so beautiful. I think I can even read for longer times without becoming weary.

It occurred to me some while ago that of all the senses that I would not want to be without, eyesight would surely hold first place. Smell, touch and hearing I could do without if necessary, but eyesight is something I use practically at every waking hour. Whether I appreciate all that, of course, is another matter. Eyesight is always there, always available whenever I need it. So, perhaps that is something to think about—namely, that those human gifts that are simply "there" are often taken for granted. But just think for a moment how intricate and complicated that human faculty and process of seeing truly is, not only the eye in and of itself, but how it is connected to the brain and how we actually see and interpret what we are seeing. It's all a great mystery—the mystery of God's creative power.

Given all that, it also needs to be said that even though we claim 20/20 vision, it could be said that we often do not truly see. Perhaps the word understand or appreciate might be a better term. I know for certain that there are many things I see every day and never think about further—even a beautiful sunset, or the face of a child, or the sight of children playing in a school yard—all beautiful sights but never reflected upon in contemplation.

I often take time to read Thomas Merton's diaries (Merton, the Trappist monk). He walked in the woods on his monastery grounds practically every day, and every day he would notice something different in nature. He would comment on the weather for that day, for instance, pointing out that it was hot and muggy, sweaty and sticky or he would point out that the trees glistened with frost. He would write about how his sandaled feet felt walking over dry leaves. He noticed things that I surely never see, all the more to my loss, of course.

Perhaps it is true to say then that all of us suffer from some sort of non-physical myopia, lack of attention, lack of insight and lack of appreciation. So much in our daily experience escapes our understanding. What is even more discouraging is that there are so many human events happening in this world every day to which we pay so little attention. Most of us read the daily newspaper or watch television news, and perhaps we will notice certain world situations that are terribly distressing. On the day I wrote this homily the morning papers' headlines told us that five more U.S. soldiers were killed in Iraq, hundreds of Kenyan people were killing each other with rocks and machetes, and Palestinian families were struggling to get across the border into Egypt so that they could buy oil, medicine and food for their families. I didn't even finish reading the articles. Isn't that interesting? I just said to myself: "Well, what can I do anyway? All that misery is on the other side of the world." Sadly, I did not even have any interior sense of compassion for those people. All this happens every day. What can you do? Well, you and I can think about it, pray about it, let it sink into our consciousness. What if any of this should happen to me?

That said, there is a story in our gospel for this Sunday about someone who did care about blindness. Jesus of Nazareth saw the seriousness of it all, and he did what he could in that situation. Jesus, obviously, did not cure everyone who appealed to him, but for whatever reason he did cure this young man. The question to ask is not "how did Jesus cure this man?" but rather "how can each of us heal like Jesus did?" Obviously, we are not miracle-workers, but perhaps we could learn better how to appreciate the humanity of the people I mentioned above, even though they may be thousands of miles apart from us. Every human person is precious in God's eyes.

If we allow Jesus to heal our blindness, the second thing we might begin to see is our overlooked population. They are the ones who are always there but often unseen, because they do not count in anyone's eyes. These are the poor, the homeless, the hungry, the out-of-work, immigrants, the under-employed, the marginalized, and the handicapped. Sometimes we are even forced to see them because they are obnoxious to us. They are always there, always disturbing our peace, always making us think.

And lastly, perhaps we could let Jesus heal our blindness if we tried deliberately to notice this day's natural beauty, whether of nature, of our work, or even of the little things we can't control—the things that disturb our peace. If we were simply to say: "Thanks, Lord, for reminding me to notice," that itself would be enough.

Finally, we must say that none of us chooses deliberately to be blind. It's just that we don't pay attention; so many other things in our lives distract us. So, the next time you do notice something so beautiful that it makes you gasp with awe and wonder, just say: "Thanks, God. Now, help me keep my eyes open to all those other things in life that are not always so beautiful but are still somehow filled with sacred meaning."

The Scriptures:
1 Samuel 16:1, 6-7, 10-13;
Ephesians 5:8-14; John 9:1-41

Year B

I suppose I should know better by now, after all the years of communicating with people, but it still amazes me how speedily and efficiently our words and our personal messages can get from one place to another and from one person to another. Just think, for instance, how quickly a little piece of gossip makes the rounds. But more to the point, any one of us who uses a computer or an ordinary cell phone will know how easily one can reach across the world. I have a good friend, a teacher who lives in the far reaches of Alaska, and we communicate by cell phone and e-mail all the time. I think I probably have around two hundred names on my e-mail address book. Now, if I were to write a letter by hand to each of these folks at Christmas time, it would be the Fourth of July before they received them.

By the way, I understand that instant messaging on cell phones is now all the rage. A friend showed me how to do it, but I found out that my fingers were too large and clumsy to cover those small keys on my cell phone. Besides, I'm sure no one could have understood my abbreviated words anyway. Ah, the fascinating world of technology. A question, however, in regard to the speed of communication is this: Does communication technology and all this messaging make us more human, more intelligent, more sensitive, more intuitive, and more responsive to others? Is our world a better place and a more humane planet because we have learned over the millennia to talk to one another? I think that may be a valid question, and I have no immediate answer.

So, it seems to me that this messaging or communicating that we do can be both good and bad. In so many cases today the message becomes less important than the means whereby the message is communicated. Our hope is that if the message gets to its destination fast, our goal will have been achieved. So, let's get the latest and fastest Intel processor!

But think about this. In the not-so-long-ago, messages

were delivered in person or delivered by a person. Someone was entrusted to get a letter or a document to an addressee. That messenger took personal responsibility to get it there. At one time in our American history, for instance, folks used the Pony Express to get a letter from point to point across the vast plains. Today, as we all know, government officials often use a personal courier to deliver top-secret documents. Even the Vatican sends important messages by courier. Whatever the case, a living person takes responsibility for delivering words, whether good or bad. If the words happen to be welcome, all the better; if unwelcome, the messenger often suffered violence or even death. Even today, we hear the phrase "to kill the messenger." It's a phrase that comes from the Greek playwright, Sophocles, in his play, *Antigone*.

But, it is not so amusing, my friends. Individuals who choose to say hard words or give warnings are often tortured or killed. We have an example in the Scriptures for this very Sunday. The Chronicler in our first reading points out that many messengers of God who were sent to the Israelites over the centuries were mistreated and their message rejected. The classic messengers in the Jewish Testament were the great prophets—Jeremiah (mentioned in today's reading), Isaiah, Micah, Ezekiel, Haggai, Malachi, and others less well known. In today's parlance, they often took the heat when they gave warnings to the people and especially to their kings. Jeremiah, for instance, was thrown into a dry cistern and left to die. He was warning the King of Israel to avoid a useless and dangerous alliance with another king.

So, you may ask, why were they persecuted? Think of it

this way. Prophets, by profession, are people who are willing to look deeply into their times and speak the truth to power. They are not willing to accept soft and easy answers for world problems, and for that they are scorned. But that is precisely the role of prophets, to ask hard questions and not allow for soft and easy answers.

Returning to the Scriptures, we know and follow the greatest prophet of all time—Jesus of Nazareth. The author of John's gospel in today's liturgy says of Jesus that he came into the world to bring light, but people preferred darkness to light, because their works were evil. How would we interpret "darkness" in our times? The common denominator in all this conflict, it seems to me, is that truth and messengers of truth will always find it difficult to get a hearing. Just think, for example, how difficult it was for Jesus to get people to listen to the Good News. Ultimately people killed the messenger.

But it seems to me too that part of our problem is that there are not enough messengers to speak truth to power. Ideally, prophets should not be in short supply in any age. Unfortunately, we imagine that it takes some special kind of person to be that messenger. Not so, I say! If we ordinary Christians are not messengers of good news, what are we good for? If we are unable or refuse to bring good news into the dark corners of our world, who will do it? This insight brings us back to our original question. What can bring true and lasting change to our world? Speedy technology or a Christian messenger who believes in the message? I think we know the answer to that. All the broadband access, all the Intel technology, all the high-powered computers, and all the cell phones in the world will never compare to one human voice who is willing to speak truth to power. Jesus did it, and so can we. May God bless you and all that you do this week.

The Scriptures:
2 Chronicles 36:14-16, 19-23;
Ephesians 2:4-10; John 3:14-21

Year C

IN THE YEAR 1992, Clint Eastwood, as the movie director, produced a film that he said would finally put to death the American Western as we have come to know it. It was entitled *Unforgiven*. It starred Mr. Eastwood himself along with Morgan Freeman and Gene Hackman—as hardened a bunch of outlaws as you might imagine. Basically, it is a story of two aged and "retired" gunslingers who decide to try out their "trade" one last time. They agree to take revenge on a local cowboy who had disfigured a prostitute. They were promised a thousand bucks if they took the job. The moral of the story is that this decision ultimately destroys them. They discover that they cannot put their past aside and turn straight; violence is too deep in their genes. Hence, they end their lives being unable to forgive themselves for their past violence. The scene I remember best comes toward the end of the film when Eastwood is lying face down in the mud of his corral sobbing over his wasted life. He feels that he is a totally useless person. His whole life had been a waste. End of story.

I think it would be true to say that there are millions of

people in the world today, especially in America, who feel that their lives have been a useless venture, and that they have never been able to shake violence out of their personality. Perhaps they feel that they have made too many mistakes to be able to redeem themselves. So, they are now on the street or in prison, living from day to day without any hope. The saddest thing of all is that they know of no one who can redeem them, give them another chance at life. A sad picture, indeed.

Several weeks ago a program appeared on National Public Television entitled "Generation Next." Judy Woodruff did interviews with young adults who had found their own way to pursue their goals in life in ways quite different than that of their parents. After some years of exploring religion and society in their own way, however, many found that they needed to return to their roots in family, school, church, et cetera. It was these roots that had originally given them roots, security, support, and a future. The point that Ms. Woodruff would make in her interviews is that exploration, testing the borders, testing the waters, and taking chances are the marks and qualities of youth and young adulthood. How can one find one's own character, one's own ego, and one's own identity unless one has the freedom to seek out life's rich possibilities?

Those of us who have some years behind us and have accumulated some wisdom in the process would say: "Fair enough, but be ready to accept the implications of what you decide to do." Of course, many of us might also say: "Don't come running back to us if you have wasted your talents and gifts. You need to live with your decisions."

The beautiful story of the Prodigal Son that we hear again on this Fourth Sunday of Lent is one of those classic stories that anyone of us could say applies to us personally as the typical story of a young person's desire for independence and its consequences. It is a narrative of a young man (of many young men or women) who want to find their own way, follow their own instincts, dictate their own terms, and to be free of the constraints of parents, home, church and society. In the process of finding his freedom, alas, the young prodigal loses his way and ultimately begins to think that there is no redemption and that he will be unforgiven. Pride and independence have gotten the best of him. But as we all know, that is not the end of the story. In all of Jesus' stories there is an out, a solution, a redemption. The young man finally saw no other solution than to swallow his pride and go home, while reciting his repentance as he walked along.

Then the scene switches to the father, who is perhaps sitting on the front porch (if he had one) shading his eyes, gazing out over the open land, wondering if his son would ever return, and what he would say if he did return. Finally, the son appears on the horizon, and the father rushes out to meet him, welcomes him, and of all things prepares a barbecue to celebrate his return.

This welcome is one of those typical endings Jesus surprises us with. This return is not the way things usually work out in life. In our hard-nosed world most of us would say: "If you want your freedom, fine; live with it, but don't come sniveling back, imagining that you can take advantage of the goodness of your friends and that everything will be forgiven and forgotten." At the same time, I think, deep in our hearts, most of us are happy with the way the story turned out. If Jesus would have had the father say, for instance: "Sonny, don't expect anything from me; you had your chance and blew it," we would not have been happy with that ending.

Well, as we all know from having listened to many of Jesus' stories, the gospel is all about redemption. They are about us, everyman and everywoman. They are about our pride, our independence, our desire to have our own way, even about our difficulty in facing our mistakes, indeed, our very selves. At the same time, in between the lines, Jesus always makes it clear that it is all right to search for our personal goals, even though they are often wrong-headed. No one is beyond redemption, no one is ever unforgiven if we want to be forgiven. That is always good to know, isn't it? Sometimes it just takes a while for each of us to grow up, but I have a hunch that God must know that too.

Maybe we should suggest to Clint Eastwood, that great movie director, that he should do a film sometime entitled *Forgiven*. That would surely be a film we could all identify with. After all, it would be all about us; we've all experienced forgiveness.

The Scriptures:
Joshua 5:9, 10-12;
2 Corinthians 5:17-21; Luke 15:1-3, 11-32

14

Fifth Sunday of Lent

†

Year A

I KNOW A RETIRED FRIEND who travels the backroads of the United States, mostly in summers, visiting small towns and trying to get a sense and flavor of the people who have immigrated here over the many years. One way he picks up this flavor of our history is by visiting cemeteries. On tombstones, he often finds epitaphs, some humorous, some serious, that give him a sense of how the relatives of the deceased thought of him or her. I'll quote just a few to give you a sense of it all. Sir John Strange: "Here lies an honest lawyer and that it is Strange is no business of yours." Or, "Here lies Lester Moore. Four slugs from a .44, no less no more." And "On the 22nd of June, Jonathan Fiddle went out of tune." Margaret Daniels: "She always said her feet were killing her. Nobody believed her." Harry Edsel Smith: Born 1903—Died 1942. "Looked up the elevator shaft to see if the car was on the way down. It was." And "Here lies an Atheist. All dressed up and nowhere to go."

So, why am I sharing all these epitaphs with you? First of

all, they are pretty funny. Sometimes the lives of the deceased are rather humorous. Even death itself, when you think about it, is sort of humorous. None of us wants to die, and yet we have no control over it. As a humorist once said: "None of us will get off this planet alive."

Part of the reason I also wanted to share these poetic verses with you is that I have a sense that none of us wants to die and be unremembered. Our relatives and friends want us to be remembered. So they print mortuary cards or long obituaries. After all, it does seem to me that every person born onto this earth was important to somebody and, hence, should be recalled, remembered, spoken well of and written well of. Of course, the deceased person has no control over that, but someone else, someone living, has that option and they often make use of it.

Epitaphs, obituaries, and eulogies also can give us a sense of the meaning of our own lives, its shortness and its tenuousness. In short, the lives of the dead are often a lesson for the living.

Well, if you have the sense that epitaphs and obituaries are a modern invention, let me point out two examples, two pieces of writing that are in the very Scriptures for this Fifth Sunday of Lent. Let me point out also that they are resurrection stories, because in our Church calendar we are nearing Holy Week and Easter. The first story or epitaph comes from the prophet Ezekiel. He has a vision where he sees scattered on the desert floor the bones of thousands and thousands of his fellow Israelites. But, in his vision he also sees these bones being reattached one to the other by the power of God. He imagines all these reattached bones springing alive and returning back to their own land. So, you see, this is a resurrection story, a prediction that death is never a total separation. Some day God will put us back together and gather us into our own land, which is the Kingdom of God.

The second epitaph or obituary story is about the only man in recorded history who died, was buried for three days, and was brought back to life. If you believe in Jesus' miracles, of course, as I do, you will have no difficulty with the details of the story. But, if you don't, then some items may puzzle you. Where was Lazarus for those three days, on earth or in heaven? Did he ever tell anyone about the experience? Did he remember anything in the grave? How did he breathe? Did his body start to decompose, as Martha feared?

Well, those are useless questions, useless because these scriptures are really more a resurrection story and not simply a story about dry bones and the dead Lazarus. Resurrection is about all of us. The power of Jesus to bring Lazarus back from the dead is the power that Jesus will bring to bear for all who believe in him.

The interesting and mysterious feature about both these readings is that they assume the reality of death but tell us nothing about what follows except to say that death is not the end. We are all destined for a life beyond this one, whether, like Lazarus, we are in the grave three days or for a millennium. The point that gives me some hope is the sense that we are all remembered. Life is precious. For many of us, someone in this world will remember us after death, even if only on a grave marker. For all of us, our God will remember us. I just can't imagine a God who has the power to create all things simply allowing us to disappear from existence...period. I still believe in resurrection, although what form it may take is still a mystery to me—perhaps to all of us.

The Scriptures:
Ezekiel 37:12-14;
Romans 8:8-11; John 11:1-45

Year B

IT'S A PECULIAR HUMAN PHENOMENON, I mean this desire many people have to "get a look at" famous people, or even better to "get to talk" to them personally. What is there about politicians, movie stars and rock stars, and sports "heroes" that makes us want to get close to them? I mean, some people (mostly teenagers) will even go so far as to rip at their clothes, try to get their autograph, et cetera. Are these people really heroes? We have to admit that some of their lifestyles leave something to be desired. EBay makes millions selling clothes and other artifacts that once belonged to famous people now long dead. It's all a great mystery to me, because I do not personally feel the need to identify with these so-called heroes, living or dead.

But, one must say something good about the folks who will spend good bucks to see a rock star or a football legend and never get any closer than a quarter of a mile away. Perhaps they simply want to admire the good human qualities of this

Fifth Sunday of Lent

person (whether they are what they appear to be or not). Perhaps it gives them a sense of pride that there are people out there who can do outstanding things and are worthy of being seen up close. In the end, we need to say that most of us are attracted by people who have done outstanding things or are at least a little better at doing certain things than we are. Hero worship has been with us for centuries, going back at least as far as we have a history of human activities. Remember, for instance, the ancient Romans and Greeks and their gods, as well as their emperor worship. So, we Americans were not the first people to discover hero worship; we've just gotten a little more sophisticated at it. Remember Pope John Paul's funeral and the election of Benedict XVI. St. Peter's Square was jammed with thousands of people for days. Obviously, we Catholics have our heroes too! What puzzles me is that heroes usually do not have much to give us, if indeed we are looking for a "handout." They are just interesting people to see!

When you hear the Scriptures for this Fifth Sunday in Lent, you will notice that Jesus of Nazareth was also a hero of sorts. Lots of people tried to get close to him, to "touch even the hem of his garment." Most of these people, of course, didn't simply want to see him, as though he were a "star"! They had learned that he was a worker of signs (miracles), that he could heal people, and that he had even raised some people from the dead. So, many people must have said to themselves: "Why not me? I'm sick too." Mysteriously, of course, we know that Jesus, for whatever reason, did not heal everyone who came to him. Nonetheless, he remained an interesting person down to the end. Even King Herod wanted to see him.

So, today in the gospel, you have an interesting little scenario about some Greek-speaking persons who wanted to see Jesus (no reason why given). Because they were not Jewish, they probably thought they didn't have a chance. So, they approached Phillip, a Greek-speaking disciple of Jesus, and asked him for an introduction. Oddly enough, however, we are never told whether they were successful or not, because Jesus immediately starts talking about something entirely different. End of the story. Great mystery! Nobody will ever know why these two Greeks wanted to talk to Jesus.

That leads us into an interesting diversion. It is true that most of us do not get to meet important persons simply by walking into their offices or homes unannounced and asking for twenty-five minutes of their time. But if we are lucky, we may be acquainted with someone who does know the famous individual personally, and he or she may be willing to give us an introduction. Sometimes it happens!

Now, the question for us today is this: How do we get to meet Jesus? Obviously, we are not going to talk to him physically, face to face. On the other hand, there are some people whom I consider very intuitive. They can speak to Jesus very openly and pray very devoutly as though Jesus were standing right in front of them. Unfortunately, I am not one of those people. It's just not that easy for me. I do pray, but not like the folks just described.

What I have found helpful for my spiritual life is to be introduced to Jesus through someone who is obviously closer to Him than I am. There are certain saints who have helped me in that—St. Francis, for one, and St. Teresa of Avila, who rode her horse around Spain to visit the nuns in her monasteries. There are others as well. Thomas Merton, the monk at Gethsemane, Kentucky, has helped me immensely to know Jesus, and I list Mother Teresa of Calcutta too. Oddly enough, there are also certain Catholic novelists and poets I have read who have also helped me receive insight into Jesus: Graham Greene, C.S. Lewis, Georges Bernanos, Flannery O'Connor, Gerard Manley Hopkins, S.J., and even some famous painters like Raphael, Giotto, Botticelli and others.

The point is that there are all kinds of people who have had some sort of relationship with Jesus who could introduce us if we were willing to listen. Of course, the best introduction to Jesus is still his own story and his life as it was lived among the people who knew him best. There is nothing better than reading and rereading the gospels, even though we may have read them lots of times before. Finally, of course, there may be no reason at all why we should need to wait for an introduction to Jesus. Perhaps the best way is simply to get brave and introduce ourselves, which is probably what we do each time we pray. If prayer is anything, it is a personal conversation with Jesus. I think we can assume that Jesus knows us, but probably does not always know what's going on in our life at this moment and might just want to hear about it. Why can't we just assume that each of us may know Jesus as well as anyone else? After all, we struck up a personal relationship with Jesus on the day we were baptized, and I suspect that has not been terminated. If news came down from the Vatican one day that Jesus would be making an appearance in our town at such and such an hour, would I go out, stand on the corner and wait to see him? You betcha! If I got close enough to say: "Hey, I know you," he would probably reply: "Hey, I know you too. How's it going?" Who needs introductions?

The Scriptures:
Jeremiah 31:31-34;
Hebrews 5:7-9; John 12:20-33

Year C

THERE ARE OCCASIONS when my errands here in Anchorage take me along a section of Third Avenue, some two miles from my office. Along that street there stands a truly unattractive building, dark grey and solidly built about five years ago. It is the municipal jail, more fittingly termed the Anchorage Correctional Facility. Whether any of the many inmates housed in that building are being "corrected" is another matter.

Nonetheless, as I drive by that building and gaze out at it, I often wonder what it must be like to be incarcerated there. Actually, I have had the occasion to visit individuals there, and each time I am escorted by a guard from the lobby into the inner "sanctum," I say to myself: "Self, consider yourself fortunate that you are not cloistered here by civil decree." I do not think I have ever done anything so heinous as to deserve being placed there, but often strange and unpredictable circumstances put people in prison. Nonetheless, just being in those small cramped quarters with no exit, save for a guard who is nowhere in sight, makes me nervous.

I have often thought how mentally difficult it must be for

prisoners to know that they will be in this place for, say, twenty-five years, or indeed a lifetime with no hope of reprieve. I am not sure how I would deal with such a circumstance. Some people commit suicide in prison. Perhaps it is because they have the sense that they can never be forgiven, indeed, that they cannot even forgive themselves. Conscience is a severe taskmaster, and the cement block walls of the building are there to remind the prisoners of their past, twenty-four/seven and three sixty-five. I often wonder how prisoners can live in such circumstances and how they live with themselves each day, knowing that tomorrow and tomorrow will be much the same as today and yesterday.

Civil society, the court system, the incarceration system, and the world at large, of course, pays little heed to the thoughts these men and women have regarding their situation. Perhaps society feels that this is not their task or responsibility. Everyone lives with their past. Given all those circumstances, I have often asked myself what can give a man or woman in prison a sense of peace with their situation. The only option I can think of is "self-forgiveness." An odd word, of course, because it does not restore justice to society. Nonetheless, despite all the circumstances of life that have put them in captivity, prisoners can come to understand that they are still good persons, worthwhile human beings, sons or daughters of God. What others may think of them is immaterial, at least in terms of their own self-image.

That long introduction was brought home to me by the lovely story (it is lovely!) about an unnamed woman in the gospel of John assigned for this Fifth Sunday of Lent. She is accused of public impropriety, prostitution or adultery. Prison was seemingly not an option. The only public option in those ancient times was capital punishment—stoning to death. Several troubling questions have consistently come to mind when reading this story. First of all, if it were truly adultery she was being accused of, what of her partner or partners? Were they not considered worthy of punishment? Why was the woman the only one being threatened with stoning? Secondly, why was a sexual offense considered so severe that it should deserve death? All sorts of crimes, many more serious than this, were doubtless committed in civil society in those times, but seemingly they did not deserve stoning to death.

The central point of this story, of course, is not the civil punishment issue but rather the human implications, and the way Jesus handled it. Obviously, the religious authorities had no concern for the woman as a human individual. They were more interested in the fact that she had publicly given religion a bad name.

Now Jesus comes on the scene and amazingly declares himself judge and jury—not in the civil sense, but in the personal and human realm. First of all, he deals with the accusers. He tells them that if any of them feel that they are sinless they may wish to throw stones. None did so. Then Jesus asks the woman the obvious follow-up question: "What happened to these other sinners?" They've disappeared," she said. "Well," Jesus says, "I guess that means that we are all sinners, just different kinds. Go in peace." That's a truly wonderful piece of drama. But the best part of it is not that Jesus forgave the woman, but that he gave her permission to forgive herself. Even if she were truly a sinner, she was obviously not the only sinner in the world.

Finally, an insight for this story comes from the first reading for today's liturgy. It comes from the prophet Isaiah. These are the beautiful words addressed to the people of his times: "Remember not the events of the past, the things of long ago consider not; see, I am doing something new...did you not notice it?" I've often wondered if Jesus might have been thinking about those very words when he told the woman to go in peace and to forget her past.

Even though most of us (I hope all of us) have never been incarcerated, we may all have a "past." None of us is perfect. The question is how do we live with our past? Do we continue to berate ourselves with our sins and shortcomings, or do we do what Isaiah says God does, namely to "remember not the events of the past, the things of long ago." If that is the way God thinks about us and invites us to forget the past, perhaps that is exactly what we should do—just forget it, period, and believe God is doing "something new" in us.

The Scriptures:
Isaiah 43:16-21;
Philippians 3:8-14; John 8:1-11

15

Palm Sunday

†

YEAR A

I IMAGINE THE IMAGE most of us have of a parade is a happy occasion commemorating some extraordinary event or accomplishment. Parades, of course, are always or usually open-air events. They happen on Broadway or on the main streets of towns and villages around the country. Everyone somehow becomes part of the parade, whether you are actually sitting in the back of a fancy car or sitting on the sidewalk watching the notables go by. We all love parades, even if we sometimes get rained on—makes no difference.

When the troops come home from Iraq, there will always be a grand reception in every small town around the country. The soldiers will be in full-dress uniform, eyes straightforward and a band will accompany them. No effort will be spared to show our thanks for these men and women who risked their lives for our country. Sometimes parades are about less serious matters, like the one that took place when the New York Giants came home the winners of the Super Bowl, or again when the Boston Red Sox won the World Series. In other words, this spectacle is the way we pay attention to certain events and heroes in our country's history. We watch, we cheer, and sometimes we also cry. It's all about showing our emotions about things we love.

But, let us also say that parades can be signs of other things as well. They can be signs of power, for instance, ways of showing that justice should be served, and that people's rights and freedoms should be respected. So, in that sense, parades or public demonstrations can be dangerous occasions. All of us can remember days when our heroes were shot. Recall John Kennedy's death in Dallas. He was a hero to many. Others will remember the day John Lennon of the Beatles was shot in New York City. He was also a hero to many. And who can forget the day that Pope John Paul II was shot in St. Peter's Square in Rome? He was a hero to Catholics and others as well. More recently we witnessed the assassination of Benazir Bhutto, the leading opposition candidate in Pakistani politics. The common thing we can say of all these individuals is that they were heroes to some, enemies to others, but especially that they were willing to take the risk of being out in public where their friends could be in touch with them. They also spoke truth to power and paid for it.

Given all that, my friends, we celebrate today the life and death of one who is truly a hero to all of us: Jesus of Nazareth. We call this day Palm Sunday of the Lord's Passion. What we remember best of this day, of course, is the blessing of the palms and the procession (parade!). It resembles the procession of Jesus into the city of Jerusalem and describes his friends, who thought him a hero and demonstrated it by laying palm branches along his path (No confetti in those days!).

The word we do not think of so often on this day, however, is Passion. We think of it more often on Good Friday, the day of the Lord's death. But I would like to think of passion in the way we think of it in daily life. We say for instance that some folks are passionately dedicated to football or some other sport. But we also say that some people are passionate about justice and peace, about abolishing the death penalty and so forth. That is the way I think of Jesus. He was passionate about honesty in God's Temple. He walked in publicly and threw out those who were cheating the poor out of their small savings. He would not allow his followers to be violent. He spoke of peace when others would take up the sword. Jesus was passionate about all of these matters. These convictions also brought him to his death. He spoke truth to power. So, that is what is so striking about that little palm procession in Jerusalem that day—a man on a donkey rides into the face of power, religious and secular, and lets power know that someone is here to do battle with it.

There is a lovely little story about Dorothy Day, the fearless peace activist. She was asked one time how Pope Pius XII could have stopped Hitler. Dorothy replied: "Well, he could have ridden into Berlin on a donkey!" Whether that would have made any difference, I do not know. But it tells you that some folks more than others have a passion for peace. That brings us to the question of what we are willing to walk for. What are we so passionate about that we are willing to stand in public and demonstrate even at the risk of our life?

So, my friends, that is what I think the Palm Sunday of the Lord's Passion is all about. It is not about waving palms and singing songs. It's about honoring and adoring our hero,

Jesus Christ, who has given us the example of what it takes to be declared a Christian. In short, it's all about risks and the courage to take them.

The Scriptures:
Isaiah 50:4-7;
Philippians 2:6-11; Matthew 26:14–27:66

Year B

THERE IS A LONG-RUNNING JOKE among Catholics that they always show up in greater numbers on Ash Wednesday and Palm Sunday, because for a change they get something back for their money! Well, to be truthful, ashes don't cost much and neither do palms. Nonetheless, it is true that Catholic folks do pack their churches on those two days along with Easter Sunday, of course. So, why is this? Well, a long time ago, Father Andrew Greeley, parish priest in Chicago, said that Catholics may have disagreements with their Church, but when push comes to shove they will never leave it because in their heart of hearts they love symbols and sacraments. It's this that keeps their faith alive for another day.

Incidentally, we do have before us this Sunday one of those occasions when Catholics do get something back, but it is not simply a few branches of palm. Let me explain. The rites and ceremonies that we will celebrate, beginning with Palm Sunday of the Lord's Passion, and including Thursday of the Lord's Supper, Friday of the Lord's Passion, the Easter Vigil, and Easter Sunday, are all rich in ritual and gesture, word and song. This week is so filled with rites that it is almost difficult to keep up with it all. (Pity the song leaders!) It is called the great Triduum, the three great days of the Lord's Pasch, his passing over from death to life and we with him in liturgy, in rite and in ritual.

There is one thing, however, that Catholics at worship need to be cautious of. All these rites are not simply play-acting. We are not trying to imitate *The Passion of the Christ*, the film we may have seen a few years ago. What we need to remember is that Jesus did, indeed, go through humiliation, suffering, pain, and human agony like none other (Remember the whipping scenes in *The Passion of the Christ*.). The question arises: What does all that pain and suffering mean to us? It happened over two thousand years ago and now it's over. Well, the answer to that is that Jesus entered into that suffering and death for our sake. The consequence is that if Christ's suffering is to have any benefit for us, we too must participate in that suffering somehow. Obviously, we cannot do that again historically with Jesus. History moves on. But there is a way to participate in Jesus' Pasch, his "passing over," and that is by entering into it by way of the liturgy. We do again, vicariously, what Jesus did once before in history.

Here is the way Patricia Sanchez, a theological scholar, puts it: "Because of Jesus' immersion in the human experience, believers may no longer regard salvation as a spiritual experience only, or as a relief that will come when death frees us from this world. Salvation is and must be a here and now experience of the mercies of God." That's really powerful.

It must also be said that Christ continues to go through his passion and death each time the human community enters into death-dealing events: wars, violence, substance abuse, disrespect for the opinions of others, et cetera. It is for these that Jesus also died. It seems only logical then that the human race, particularly the followers of Jesus, should join in this effort to reduce the power of evil in our time and make repentance for our participation in the world's fallen-ness. The end of all this, of course, is Easter Sunday of the Lord's Resurrection. As Paul says: "If we die with Him (Christ), we shall also live with him."

Given all that, therefore, it will be worth our while to pass with Christ from Palm Sunday to Easter Sunday. The rewards will be greater than a few palms that often enough are left to dry somewhere and to be forgotten. But aren't those ceremonies so long? Yes, indeed, they are long, but on Easter Sunday we will be able to say to ourselves: "I was there with Christ in his suffering; now I rise with Him in glory."

The Scriptures:
Isaiah 50:4-7; Philippians 2:6-11; Mark 14:1–15:47

YEAR C

I IMAGINE MOST FOLKS HERE this evening can remember around the time of Holy Week, when Mel Gibson's film, *The Passion of the Christ*, first hit the theaters. The very timing of its opening, of course, already tells you something. Mel Gibson is no dummy. At any rate, it was a popular film, despite the terrible violence it depicted. People still flocked to it, including entire church congregations at reduced ticket rates, of course. *The*

Passion of the Christ was probably the first film produced that actually portrayed capital punishment in all its ugliness. As Catholics, we have all seen and made our Stations of the Cross, but in terms of violence, they are nothing in comparison to Gibson's film. Perhaps, for the first time, we saw violence the way it actually took place in the days of the Roman Empire. Historians tell us that every crucifixion attracted crowds of people, and the Romans made sure that it was handled as a public spectacle so that other would-be criminals might think twice before carrying out their deeds.

Why other ordinary folks would choose to come and view such a display of cruelty, however, is a mystery. The gladiator games at the Forum in Rome, of course, always attracted thousands as well. Some in the United States today say that Sunday afternoon NFL football is not much different, but at least players don't usually get killed. At any rate, down through history public executions have attracted the curious and the prurient. Witness the executions during the French Revolution, the ethnic "cleansing," between Hutus and Tutsis, and even those old black and white photos that show public hangings of African-American slaves here in the United States during the late 1800s. Families—mom, dad and the kids—are all present watching the Sunday afternoon spectacle! Or, why, for instance was there so much interest worldwide at the gruesome hanging of Saddam Hussein and his cohorts? For some reason the suffering and death of individuals has always attracted people. It seems a great mystery to me, but it happens.

The parallel I am about to draw now may not seem very appropriate, but Catholics and many Christian denominations witness a public execution twice each year, once on Palm Sunday and again on Good Friday. Obviously, we do not think of it in those terms. After all, this is Holy Week, the holiest time of the liturgical year, when we remember the suffering, death, and resurrection of Jesus Christ. We do not think of ourselves as witnessing an execution. We have heard the narration of the Passion so many times that it has lost much of its original violence for us. Nonetheless, Jesus did suffer and die publicly. It was the worst kind of execution one could imagine, worse even than hanging.

What should we be thinking of then as we listen to the Passion account again this year? Perhaps the only way to get some personal sense of it is to think of ourselves as standing along the street where Jesus passed, or standing at a distance on the bottom of Calvary Hill watching the entire spectacle of an innocent and good man being put to death. But still, does that give us a sense of its meaning in terms of present-day circumstances in the world?

We have all read the phrase in our catechisms, which we recite in the Creed, that Jesus "died for us and for our salvation." Theologically, that is true: Jesus died for us, and not for us as an anonymous group of people, but for us individually and personally. There is also another way, however, one might think of the death of Jesus, namely as a metaphor or a model for the ways unjustified suffering and death are still carried out among us today. I think, for instance, of the number of people in the United States who have been executed by mistake. I think of the history of violence against Black Americans during the civil-rights movement in the South, and the murder and disfiguration of the young Black man, Emmett Till. They said he had whistled at a white lady. I think of the American nuns and lay missionaries who were murdered by military personnel in El Salvador: Dorothy Kazel, Jean Donovan, Maura Clarke and Ita Ford. I think too of Archbishop Oscar Romero, who was martyred as he celebrated a public Mass. All of these folks and many others in modern history were crucified, not precisely like Jesus was crucified, but they died nonetheless in their efforts to bring peace and justice to others.

All that in mind perhaps will help us listen more attentively each Palm Sunday and Good Friday when we hear the gospel of the Passion read again. True, it did happen but once in history, but it continues to happen each time one of Jesus' brothers or sisters dies an undeserved death. One thing is for sure. We cannot passively stand on the side of the street looking on as these things happen to others. There is too much at stake.

The Scriptures:
Isaiah 50:4-7;
Philippians 2:6-11; Luke 22:14–23:56

16

Holy Thursday

✝

Some years ago I had the opportunity to celebrate the marriage of two young folks of our parish, both Catholic, and both having made their way through our religious formation program. I never thought of them as particularly pious, just ordinary young teenagers who had made their way into adulthood and were now prepared to enter the mysterious world of Holy Matrimony. I helped them prepare the marriage liturgy, choose the readings, prayers and all the rest. When I asked them whether there was anything in the Scriptures they might want me to reflect on for the homily, they said: "Well, Father, if you don't mind, we'd like to do the homily ourselves." I said, "Ok by me, just keep it under a half-hour if you can."

When the day of the wedding came around, I began to wonder what they planned on saying in the homily. Priests always worry about stuff like that. This is usually the time for the presider to get in a few choice words about marriage and family matters. Actually, I already had some sense of what they might want to say, because they had selected the Last Supper event in the gospel of John, the very one which we just read a few moments ago. So, the gospel was read and everyone sat down, waiting for the homily. Not a word! Dead silence! Much to my astonishment, the couple just sat at their chairs and began taking off their shoes and socks. Then two of the wedding attendants brought up a bowl of water and a towel and placed them at the couples' feet.

Well, you already know the rest: There was no homily, not in the normal sense. Each of them in turn simply got up and washed each other's feet, wiped them and sat down. End of story! Not a word, no homily, no explanation, no reasons given. In other words, the action took the place of anything they might have said. Then there was a period of total silence as they replaced their shoes and socks, and their parents and friends sat there with their mouths open! I'd have to say, however, that it was probably one of the best wedding homilies I had ever heard or seen! Of course, it could have turned out to be a big show, something to impress their friends with their personal piety. But this was not the case. They simply wanted to say or do something that would be a sign of their dedication to one another. I'm sure they are probably still happily married, and perhaps they are also still washing one another's feet, at least I hope that is the case.

All this tells me that sometimes, oftentimes, actions are more effective than words. Indeed, this is what St. James said in his letter to the early Christians: "Be doers of the word and not hearers only." We have just listened to a dramatic reading of another incident of foot-washing. No doubt, we have heard that reading many times and may have let it go at that. This loving care is just what Jesus usually did—something astonishing, something different. He was always doing such things.

But think about this: This was the evening of the Paschal Supper, one of the most important feasts in the entire Jewish calendar. It was all about story-telling, and about eating and drinking in memory of Jewish history. There was no rubric in the ceremony about foot-washing, none whatsoever. Everyone must have been totally amazed when Jesus turned this ancient and sacred ceremony into something personal like this. Didn't history count for anything?

My sense of the foot-washing ceremony is this. Jesus might have said to himself: "Here's my chance to do something important." So, he might well have said to them: "My friends, now that I have you all together, perhaps for the last time, let me share a word or two with you. Did you understand what I just did for you? You address me as 'Teacher' and 'Lord' and fittingly enough, for that is what I am. But, if I washed your feet—I who am Teacher and Lord—then you must wash one another's feet. What I just did was to give you an example: as I have done, so you must also do."

What's this all about? Well, what it is all about is Jesus' insistence that his disciples who wish to be his followers need to learn how to be servants to one another. There is nothing more fundamental than that about being Christian. In other words, we can talk all day about how we love one another, but unless we are willing "to get down on our knees" and be servants to one another, it will mean very little. Actions speak louder than words. So, how does all this break out in the context of our everyday life? Obviously, we are probably not actually going to be washing one another's feet literally every day. We are pretty sensitive about how our feet look anyway. We'd prefer not to touch someone else's feet! But, we do need to demonstrate what foot-washing means. We do need to be servants to one another, and to do so not in a demeaning way, but in total integrity and truthfulness. It could mean something like this: Be honest with one another; no phoniness. It could mean speaking respectfully to one another. It could mean putting up with one another's annoying and irritating habits. Even more, it could mean having to do what we don't always like doing—all for the sake of others. Actually, it's all contained in those lovely words of the marriage ceremony—love and honor one another, especially in circumstances of riches and poverty, sickness and health, difficulties or joys, day in and day out. That's what serving one another should mean.

In a few moments we shall once again participate in that ancient ceremony. There is always the chance, as in so many other liturgical ceremonies, that it will seem like just another ritual formality that we Catholics are so well known for. We have to be careful of theatrics. Truly, what happens after this rite is over, what happens at home, at work or wherever, tomorrow and the day after, will be what ultimately counts. If we have not learned the everyday meaning of this rite, then perhaps it would be better that we not do it at all.

Getting on our knees is not something we do easily. It's a long way to the floor. Being servants to one another is never easy or simple either. We have to keep learning and doing it over and over again. If tonight is the time we decide to start over again, then all we do here will have been worthwhile.

The Scriptures:
Exodus 12:1-8, 11-14;
1 Corinthians 11:23-26; John 13:1-15

17

Easter Sunday

†

A Personal Experience

BACK IN THE YEAR 1960, Federico Fellini, the famous Italian movie director, produced a film called *La Dolce Vita* (the sweet life). It was a critical commentary on the decadent life of the rich and famous in Rome. The film opens with a scene of a helicopter flying around and around over the city of Rome. To it, attached by ropes, was a huge cement statue of Jesus Christ, arms outstretched and looking down on the city. People down below are all staring up in the sky saying: "Hey, look, Jesus has come back. What do you think that could mean?" Well, after a while the helicopter, with Jesus in tow, disappears off in the distance over the edge of the city and the people down below in Rome soon forget about the experience and go back to what they were doing before Jesus first appeared. The rest of the film then traces the lives of various people whose lifestyles did not change very much despite the fact that Jesus had come back to the city.

It's pretty obvious that Fellini is making a statement on the impact of Jesus' coming into the world. The question is:

What does that mean to people? I have always thought of that film as a kind of resurrection story, Jesus returning to earth and then asking what that means to us, if indeed he should return.

So, that is the question. If Jesus were to return, whether by helicopter or on his own power, what could that mean for those of us who are Christian? Would the world be any different if we knew that Jesus Christ would come swooping down over our city someday? That may sound like a crazy question, but I think most of us do believe that Jesus is still present in the world in some way, and that his resurrection has made it possible for him to be eternally present with us.

It seems to me, then, that this brings up some questions for us to consider on this Easter morning. The first question is this: If we do believe that Jesus Christ is still present with us, how does that happen and what does it mean? The second question is this: Does it do much good for us simply to sit around thinking about Jesus' resurrection, whether at Easter or at any other time? Or again, does it do any good simply to think of Jesus' resurrection as something that only happened to him? In other words, is there such a thing as a personal experience of resurrection, and not simply the experience of a truth or a doctrine, important as that might be? What would that mean? How would it feel? How would we know it is even happening? The point is this: If the resurrection of Jesus Christ cannot be a personal experience, then it is hardly worth coming here today to sing our Alleluias. That is my conviction.

So, back to our first question: How is Jesus Christ still living and present in the world today? Let me introduce that with a story from another film from the year 1977, this time by the Italian film-maker Franco Zeffirelli. It was titled *Jesus of Nazareth*. The story goes like this: Jesus has been crucified and is hastily buried. Soon thereafter a member of the Jewish Sanhedrin is informed by a messenger that certain followers of this itinerant preacher, Jesus, were spreading the news that Jesus' tomb had been found empty, and that his followers were now claiming that they could still experience him present among them in some mysterious way. At that, the Jewish Temple official closed his eyes, took a deep breath, sighed and said: "Well, so it begins again. It all begins again." A great insight if we look at it historically. How little did he know that his words were actually to come true. That, in fact, is exactly what has happened. Jesus is still present in some mysterious, but real way. The resurrection of Jesus marks a new way of life for millions and millions of people down through history. I would like to think that this is the very reason why we are here this morning. We are part of that crowd of millions and millions down through history who believe Jesus is still present when we gather like this, Sunday after Sunday, to remember him as he asked his disciples (and us) to do when he celebrated his last supper with them. The point is, when Christians come together, Jesus comes to life again and again. Resurrection happens again in the flesh and blood of his followers, all of us here today. If that is not the case, then I would be hard pressed to know what we are, in fact, doing here.

 The second question is this: Is the resurrection simply a church doctrine, a phrase in the Nicene Creed, something to puzzle over, to ask how it could ever have happened? Or is it, must it somehow be, an individual experience, even aside from our gathering here Sunday after Sunday? Have any of you ever had a resurrection experience? I obviously do not mean a rising from the grave, but something you could describe as life beginning all over again today. In other words, can resurrection be personal? That is the central question about Easter.

But, you may say, how would I know that? How would it happen? Well, first of all, I think we would need to say that there is a difference between resurrection and immortality. Immortality simply means never dying. Resurrection, on the other hand, is a daily experience, something that is actually happening, something personal you could describe as worth getting up for in the morning. That's resurrection! So, what are some examples of that? Well, have you ever known people of whom you could say that this person is always full of life, always happy, always hopeful, and always ready to find something good to say, even though things may not always go consistently well? That's a resurrection experience. Or have you ever personally had a bout with some sickness over a long period of time, perhaps even being confined to the hospital, and then finally being told by your doctor that you are cured and healthy again and can go home? That's the feeling of resurrection. Or when two people, for instance, who dearly love one another but have had a falling out, decide to put their differences aside and love one another again—that's the experience of resurrection. Or, do you have a natural taste for beauty, for goodness, and for truth? If you do, that's a resurrection experience. Can you manage to find something good to say about even depressing situations? That's resurrection. Are you moved by the smile on a child's face, a good joke or some really humorous situation? That's resurrection. Something has transformed your life and brought you happiness.

The point of all this is to say that resurrection is happening all the time. It's going on at this very moment if we are aware enough to notice it, whether within ourselves or in the world around us. Resurrection, in other words, is dynamic; you should be able to notice it when it is happening.

Finally, I think we should say that Jesus probably will not come back today to this city, whether by helicopter or by any other means. But we would also need to say that he has actually never left this world. That Jewish religious official we talked about earlier was so right: "And so it begins," he said, and it does begin again today, tomorrow, and every day when we decide that the spirit of Jesus never dies. It can burst forth in a million different ways in the lives of people like us, people who are convinced, as Bishop Fulton Sheen used to say, that "life is worth living." If life is not worth living, then there is no resurrection—simple as that.

The Scriptures:
Acts 10:34, 37-43; Colossians 3:1-4; John 20:1-9

How Many Years Was Easter Sunday?

I CAN REMEMBER A CONVERSATION I had with a lady some years ago around this time of year and she was saying to me: "You know, it's really a shame what they have done to Easter." By "they" I assumed that she meant the commercial or the advertising world, or some such entity. So, I said to her, "What do you mean by 'what they've done to Easter'?" She said: "Well, you know, all those silly things like Easter bunnies, Easter egg searches for the kids, women wearing silly-looking hats only on Easter Sunday, Easter ham, Easter bread, Easter candy, all that stuff." I said: "Well, it's true, but look what they have also done to Christmas." But then I went on to say to her: "I think there might be something behind all these customs that people don't realize at first. Odd as it may sound, I think it has something to do with resurrection. We have never been able to figure out exactly what Jesus' resurrection means; so, instead, we try to find natural human symbols or customs that speak about it. I think that's what it's all about. When you are faced with mysteries, you always depend on symbols, simplistic as they may sound, to help you understand what you don't understand."

So, what is Easter all about? What are Easter eggs and chocolate bunnies and flowered hats all about? Well, strange as it may sound, these symbolic actions are about the human inclination, indeed the eternal longing, for everlasting life. They are about resurrection, not necessarily Jesus' resurrection only, but all our resurrections, the belief that all of us were created for eternal life. If that's not the case, what are we doing here this morning; why do we "go to Mass" every Sunday; indeed, why do we even get up out of bed in the morning at all?

Perhaps one of the things that make it so hard for us to understand the experience of resurrection is that we have the sense that this was a miracle—this was something that God did for Jesus alone, because Jesus is literally the Son of God. So, resurrection is often seen as a special gift or privilege for God's only Son, whereas it was actually meant for all of us.

Resurrection is such a mystery for us because we may think of it as "resuscitation," that is, the raising up of a dead body, the deceased body of Jesus. But there is a difference between resuscitation and resurrection. One scripture scholar put it this way: "Resuscitation never happened. Resurrection always happens." Resuscitation means that a dead body is brought back to life, only to die again someday. Resurrection means that Jesus died physically, but continues to live with us, not in a physical, bodily sense but, as the theologians say, in his glorified body—a body that transcends time and place, a body that can be experienced without flesh and blood. In other words, if Jesus Christ meant to be with us until the end of time, then a physical body would not be the means whereby he would be able to do this. Jesus lived in a physical body just like we do. But physical bodies simply are not built or created to live forever. But that does not mean that we do not want to live forever. If I were to ask any of you individually whether you want to live forever, you would say: "Absolutely; I can't imagine living, then dying and passing out of existence forever. Why was I created in the first place, if just to live for a few short years and then die and be forgotten?" That's a pretty depressing thought, and none of us believes it, I'm sure.

So, even though none of us really understands everlasting life, we long for it and believe that it does happen. For instance, why do we continue working at our jobs every day, even though they are boring and don't always seem to have much future? Why do we struggle to maintain our good health every day? Why do we plan for our future and our children's future if this world is all there is? Why do we dream about better days when we fall ill? In short, we all say to ourselves: "If God could raise

Jesus Christ from the dead, why not me? Why should I be left out of the loop? I want to live forever too."

The point, therefore, is that there is nothing wrong with searching for signs and symbols which seem to speak to us about eternal life. Is that not why we listen attentively to the Scriptures each Sunday when they are proclaimed? Is that not what receiving the sacred bread and cup at Eucharist means? Or again, on a less theological level—why is it that parents are so delighted at the birth of their first child? Isn't it because they now know that there is a future of some kind for their family, if not eternal, then at least for now, for an "earthly-moment"?

There is an interesting line in the gospel for this Easter day. Mary Magdalene comes to the tomb and does not find the body of Jesus. She goes back to the apostles and says: "They have taken the body of my Lord and I do not know where they have laid Him." Mary obviously thought that someone had absconded with the physical body of Jesus, and that she would never see him again. And yet, we know that Mary and the other disciples continued to experience Jesus on a number of occasions later on, albeit in rather mysterious ways: Entering through a locked door, preparing breakfast on a beach, to name two. In other words, Jesus continued to be with them in a different, non-physical way. It took an act of faith to understand all that, of course.

So, Mary Magdalene's complaint that she did not know where they had laid the body of Jesus should not be our complaint. We may not know where the physical body of Jesus lies (it doesn't lie anywhere), but we should surely know where the Mystical Body of Christ lives each day. It walks in our own feet, in the feet of the Body of Christ, the Church. It walks wherever love and healing and teaching and feeding and compassion and care are going on. In short, resurrection always happens. It keeps on happening wherever we try to make Christ present again and again. In a sense, the resurrection-life of Jesus Christ continues, because he depends on us to make it present in our world today.

"Wow," you will say, "that's a huge responsibility!" True enough, but ultimately it is easier to believe in the power of the resurrection than in the meaning of bunny rabbits and chocolate eggs! So, when someone asks you how many years was Easter Sunday, you can tell them, "Don't start counting; Easter is for ever and so are we."

The Scriptures:
Acts 10:34, 37-43; Colossians 3:1-4; John 20:1-9

18

Second Sunday of Easter

†

Year A

On occasion as I begin Mass on a typical Sunday, I ask myself: "Is this the way Jesus would do what I'm doing?" If Jesus decided to come back to any typical Catholic parish on a given Sunday morning, would he or his early disciples still recognize what we are doing to be what Jesus did at the Last Supper or what those early Christians did in their little communities described in the Acts of the Apostles? Probably not, at least in some of the details that we follow today.

But does it make any difference? History, as we know, moves on. Everything changes over periods of time, even something as sacred and transcendent as the Mass. Nonetheless, it is interesting to imagine what Jesus, from his place in God's kingdom, must think about what has transpired in the Church over two thousand years. We Christians surely hope that we have not taken too many liberties with those words Jesus used and the basic actions Jesus performed at the Last Supper. The better question to ask, of course, is not what would Jesus think if he were to walk into our worship space some Sunday morning, but rather, can we typical Sunday morning Catholics recognize Jesus in our churches as the early Christians recognized him after the resurrection?

I think there are two ways to answer that question and the answers are in the Scriptures for this Second Sunday in Easter season. The first answer comes from the Acts of the Apostles, the book that describes what those early Christian communities looked like. The first thing you will notice is that they were not Mega Churches where three or four thousand folks gathered. They were simply small gatherings of perhaps a couple dozen families from the same neighborhood where everyone knew each other and surely felt committed to each other. They were poor and rich, famous and not so famous, even of different nationalities.

How does that compare to the Church, the Christian community, we are part of? Can I find Jesus present in that person sitting next to me, even though I may not know his or her name or even recognize his different nationality? After all, we both go by the name Christian, do we not? That should be enough to bond us into the community of Jesus.

Second, that reading from Acts says that the early Christians celebrated the Eucharist in a very simple way. They devoted themselves to the breaking of the bread and to prayers. They also shared what common goods they had. So, the question: Despite how different our Church looks today, despite all the elements that have been added to our liturgy over the years, can we still recognize Jesus in this community? Can we find him again in the simple act of the breaking of bread and prayers?

The third element mentioned in that reading is that those

Second Sunday of Easter

early Christians were a happy lot. They "ate their meals with exultation"! The question is: How happy do we seem to be on a typical Sunday? Do these Christians gathering for the ten o'clock Mass look like they believe in the resurrection? Could a stranger recognize them as joyful people if he or she happened to drift in on a Sunday morning? I realize, of course, that a lot of history has happened in our Church over the years, but my point is that it would be a nice idea for all of us to compare ourselves to those early Christians, perhaps even to simplify our worship so that Jesus would continue to become evident to us when we gather.

Now we turn to that nice little story of Thomas, "the doubter," who had such a hard time being convinced that it was still the same Jesus he met on that day after Jesus' death and resurrection. I have always had a certain compassion for Thomas. He refused to take things for granted. He knew that Jesus had been killed, and now he is told that Jesus is still living! It might take a lot to convince any of us that a friend of ours, whom we knew had died, has suddenly reappeared alive. "Give me proof," we'd say, just as Thomas said: "Let me touch, please."

It's so easy, of course, two thousand years after the event to say: "What's the matter with this guy? What should it take to convince him?" Remember, however, we have two thousand years of reflection on all this and lots of theology. It's so easy for us to simply say: "Hey, just believe; it's ok."

The more important question to ask, however, is not the one about Thomas, but rather to ask: Is our faith in the risen Jesus strong enough to find him not in the flesh or the wounds as Thomas was asked to do? Rather the question to ask is this:

Can we still find Jesus in the symbols that the early Church has left us—those signs that say Jesus is present in a human way, but not necessarily in the flesh?

How much of an effort do we make, for instance, to pay careful attention to the Gospel, the words of Jesus, as they are proclaimed on a Sunday? Has the Mass and the Eucharist gotten a little "threadbare" for us over the years, a little "same-old" after having celebrated it Sunday after Sunday? Like those early Christians, can we still get excited about coming together on Sunday? Are we still convinced that it is worth the effort to throw our whole being into this one wonderful hour of prayer? Can we allow these sacred moments simply to become the "same-old, same-old" week after week?

Finally, like Thomas the Apostle, perhaps we should insist that all we are really hoping for during that hour on Sunday is to be back in touch with Jesus. It worked pretty well for Thomas. With a little effort, it should work for us too.

The Scriptures:
Acts 2:42-47; 1 Peter 1:3-9; John 20:19-31

Year B

I AM NOT ORDINARILY much of a "Prime Time" TV watcher. There are too many good books and periodicals to read. But once in a while, for a change, I may watch "CSI" (Crime Scene Investigation) or one of those other murder investigations. The work of those investigators always seems pretty professional—

Second Sunday of Easter 163

the way it's probably done in so-called "real life," whatever that may mean. What strikes me about those programs is the attention they pay to bodily evidence to solve the crime—little things that anyone other than a forensics expert would probably miss entirely. In short, the body, dead or alive, can tell you a lot simply by looking at it.

Of course, we all know a little something about our own body and body language. Our bodies speak volumes. People, for instance, can tell in a moment by looking at us how we are feeling, sad or happy, worried or complacent. We can't help it; our body gives us away. Look around, for instance, in church, when the Sunday homily is going on a bit longer than usual. People get "antsy," they shuffle around in their seats, and they are getting impatient. If the preacher notices that, he may decide to terminate his remarks in a hurry. People have probably stopped listening anyway. The point I am making is that the body communicates whether we notice it or not. For CSI investigators, even dead bodies communicate something.

Another way of communicating, as we all know, is by word of mouth. It's the primary method for us humans to be in touch with someone. One of the main factors that make this kind of communication possible is the assumption that whoever is talking to us is telling us the truth. If we cannot depend on that, then the world is in real trouble!

Of course, we all know that a lot of lying goes on every day, especially in the political arena (good word!). Seldom, of course, will anyone admit to lying; it's a bad word. No one will even admit to "wrongdoing." That's also too incriminating. But for the most part we do depend on the truthfulness of others to carry on the world's business and our personal business as well. It's the only option we have and it's a good one.

What all this comes down to is the fact that we are all flesh and blood beings in this world. Everything depends on what we can see, touch, feel and hear. For the most part, we always trust our senses. They can tell us a lot. As we all know, we also depend a lot on material things out there to tell us something. It's all about symbolism, sign and language. We who are Catholic know all about that. Our churches are filled with statues and stained-glass windows depicting sacred images. Our sacraments make sense only because they are material signs of the sacred. We can learn a lot about our faith simply by walking into a church and looking, listening, even smelling the incense used in rituals.

All I've been saying then is meant to lead us to an understanding about discovering Jesus again, but in signs. That is what the season of Easter is all about, discovering the risen Jesus Christ today. The gospel story today about Thomas the Apostle and his problem believing that Jesus was still alive is one of those classical examples of believing in the flesh. Now, let us not assume that Thomas was simply not too bright or that he had to have hard-edged proof for everything. Any of us who have been present at a funeral are obviously convinced that what we are "viewing" is a deceased person. This was Thomas's problem. He knew clearly that Jesus had been subject to capital punishment. He died on a cross. To be asked to believe then that Jesus was still alive was something of a stretch. So, I suggest that Thomas was not so much a doubter or a cynic as he has always been portrayed in Christian history. He simply wanted physical proof that his assumptions were wrong, and that Jesus was still alive.

So, what happens? Two things: First, the other apostles say

to him: "Take our word for it, Thomas, he's still alive." Then, seven days later when the whole group is together again, Jesus himself appears, and says in effect: "Thomas, if you could not take the word of your friends about me, here take your finger and trace the wounds on my body. That should clear up all your doubts." And, of course, we know the end of the story. Thomas, moved to faith in Jesus' body, was convinced he was still in touch with the Jesus he once knew "in the flesh."

Now, this story and the others you will hear in the next few weeks of Easter season are not just little pieces of history. They are what we call pieces of theology, stories to help us to believe. It's not that we are all a bunch of doubters. But, trying to be a believing Christian is not an easy thing. Everything we read in the gospels about Jesus we accept on the word of others. Everything we believe depends on the truthfulness of our history and on human persons who have passed it all down to us. That may all sound like a pretty tenuous stretch to make, but it's literally all we have. As I mentioned above, all our relations with each other depend on the words we share, even our body language, our truthfulness in searching for the meaning of life.

Finally, the gospel writer who handed this story of Thomas on to us ends his gospel with a beautiful little piece of explanation. He wants to tell us why he went to all the trouble to pass on the story of Jesus. Here is what he says: "Jesus performed many other signs as well—signs not recorded here—in the presence of his disciples. But these have been recorded to help you believe that Jesus is the Messiah, the Son of God, so that through this faith you may have life in his name." What he is saying is this: "Friends, I have put all this down on paper because I know that you who read this down through the centuries may have a hard time believing it. I'm just telling you what I saw and heard—all those signs Jesus left us. It's all to help you believe that Jesus was who he said he was, the Son of God. Take my word for it. I'm still trying to figure it all out myself."

The Scriptures:
Acts 4:32-35;
1 John 5:1-6; John 20:19-31

Year C

As a priest I think a lot about Jesus. I hope that doesn't sound odd! I guess we all think a lot about Jesus. It's a normal thing for Christians and Catholics to do. After all, our entire Catholic life of faith is wrapped up in the one we call Son of God, our Lord, the Messiah.

Of course, there is also a lot we don't know about Jesus. The gospel writers never meant to write a full biography of Jesus' life. They are sketchy at best. Moreover, they come to us through the courtesy of those little Christian communities we call the "early church," the ones mentioned in the Acts of the Apostles and the reading from the Book of Revelation in today's readings. Each of them had a slightly different memory of Jesus that they wanted to pass on to us to keep our faith alive even in this the Twenty-first Century. The point is that our Christian faith depends in great part on what we have heard and learned from others. The church of history passes on its faith from one generation to the next.

Another question that often comes to my mind, especially on a Sunday morning when we are all gathered together like this, is whether our church, this one here and now, resembles what Jesus had in mind when he said: "On this rock I will build my church." The church that quickly grew up after Jesus' resurrection was basically Middle Eastern, Jewish and Gentile—the cultures and religions of that time. Today, there may be a dozen or more different nationalities and languages gathered for Mass on a typical Sunday morning. Look around! Did Jesus think about that and did the early apostles think that the Church would eventually look like it does today? It may not seem like an important question, because we assume that the Church, like other organizations, grows with history.

The point I am trying to come to is that our Christian faith depends heavily on many human factors. We learn that, first of all, from the story of Thomas the Apostle in today's gospel. Some people over the centuries have called him a doubter, but my sense is that Thomas was truly a man of faith. He obviously had spent some time with Jesus of Nazareth. He had known him personally and physically. He also knew that Jesus died in the flesh (as Paul says). So, when Thomas's friends tell him that they have seen Jesus, he wants proof, and the only proof he thought he could accept would be to actually touch the physical body of Jesus. That would be proof enough. I'm sure any of us, given the same situation, would have said the same thing: "Give me proof!"

The fact is, of course, that we depend on material things all the time for proof of what we are searching for. We want to know, for instance, to whom we are talking on the phone; we want to know whether the photo we are looking at represents the person whose name appears on the bottom. If a friend of a blind person says, "This is a flower," the blind person may say, "Let me touch it," or "Let me smell it." In other words, we humans are so dependent upon our senses that we just have to put our trust in them. We have no other option. Usually, they do not deceive us.

My point here is that, as Catholics, as worshipers in Church each Sunday, we are much in the same position as Thomas was. We want to know about Jesus. That's why we are here. But, to be in touch with Jesus we depend on some very human factors—our sense of sight, of hearing, of touch, even of smell. We taste bread and wine, and we believe it to be the body and blood of Christ. We make an act of faith. We smell the rich odor of incense and believe that our prayers also rise up to God's sight. We hear lovely organ music, or a choir, and our faith is given meaning by it. We look around and see each other sitting here and we say: "Look, that person believes in Jesus like I do. That's a great source of faith for me. We all believe together."

Finally, we are all faced with a great mystery when we talk about faith. We say, "I believe," and we hope we are doing the right thing, because we depend so much on simple human factors. In the end, our goal is not absolute surety. Like Thomas, it's about trust, trust that God will not deceive us.

St. Anselm of Canterbury, a great theologian of the Middle Ages, once said that theology, that is, the search for God, is "faith seeking understanding." I think that is the reason why we are here today—believers all seeking understanding. Remember too what St. Paul once said to his parishioners: "We see now as though through a glass, darkly, but then (someday) face to face." Perhaps that's about all we can ask for now, just to see God even darkly, but with the promise that someday it will be clearly face to face.

The Scriptures:
Acts 5:12-16;
Revelation 1:9-13, 17-19; John 20:19-31

19

† Third Sunday of Easter

Year A

ONE OF THE COMFORTING things about being a presider at Mass is that you have a sense that you are in charge! I don't mean for that to sound disrespectful, but when you are standing before, say, a couple hundred people who have come to church to experience God or the sacred, you know that you have a serious responsibility on your hands. People expect you to know what you are doing and to help them celebrate the liturgy in a reasonably sacred manner. That's your job! Let me point out, however, that, as in other activities in life, arrangements do not always run smoothly, even those we consider sacred.

Let me tell you, for instance, where things can get really messy at Mass, and where you sometimes can lose control. It's mainly at the time of the distribution of Holy Communion. Don't misunderstand me. Folks are ordinarily quite orderly at Communion time; however, it's the moms and dads who are "dragging" their little kids along—that's where I sometimes lose control. Kids are really funny (they don't know it, of course). Often when they come before me, they will say:

"Hey, are you really God?" Or, "Are you Jesus?" More often though they will extend their stubby little hand or grab hold of the ciborium with the sacred hosts and say: "I want some of that too." At that point the mother or father will say: "You don't get any yet, come on, let's go," and they get dragged off. Then the crying begins, of course, and I know well that at this point I have truly lost all control of the situation. But, who can blame the kids? Everybody else is "getting Jesus" except these little guys and girls. I'd be mad too if I didn't "get something" at Communion time. Who can blame them?

In some mysterious way, I'm sure most Catholics when they come to church are asking for exactly what the little kids are asking for. If they could explain it, they would want to say: "I had an experience of God today." How that happens, of course, is a great mystery. Each person experiences God in a unique manner. Fundamentally, however, whether we happen to be at Mass or not, we instinctively want to be in touch with the sacred.

That is exactly the situation we find in the gospel for this Sunday, which tells the beautiful story of the two followers of Jesus who had the sacred experience of meeting Jesus Christ and didn't even know who he was. Purely by accident they meet him on their way home to Emmaus soon after the terrible days of the crucifixion. They have no idea who this stranger is, but they strike up a conversation with him about all that has happened in Jerusalem during those past few days. It was sad news for them, obviously, but they had to say it. At last the stranger says: "Here, let me explain what all this means. Have you never read the Scriptures? All that just happened was predicted by the prophets." The disciples, of course, still have no idea with whom they are speaking and no idea that this man is talking about himself.

Finally, they reach a hotel; the day is late, so they invite the stranger to have supper with them. He doesn't seem all that interested but finally says, "Ok." In the middle of the supper he takes a piece of bread, breaks it and hands it to them. They probably had a cup of wine too, although it's not mentioned. All of a sudden they say: "Hey, wait a minute, we've seen all this before. Remember the Last Supper?" At that point they know for sure they are talking with Jesus. It's the Last Supper all over again.

The question is how did they know it was still the same Jesus? Jesus did not introduce himself. Two things are clear from the past. First, Jesus explained the Scriptures and then he broke bread with them. It is probably safe to say that this was one of the first times, after the Last Supper, that Mass was celebrated.

Now, why are we hearing all this? We are hearing all this in the Scriptures because the early Christians, our brothers and sisters, wanted everyone to know that you could recognize Jesus if you came together as a community, read and shared the Scriptures and then broke bread together. In simplest form, that is what we do each Sunday.

So now let's go back to the Holy Communion stories I told earlier. If you ask practically any Catholic to name what is most important to them while celebrating Mass together, they will say: "When we receive Holy Communion; that is where we meet Jesus Christ." The problem with that answer is that we are missing part of the picture. Jesus actually became recognizable to those early Christians in several ways: First, by gathering the folks; second, by explaining the Scriptures; third, by breaking bread and sharing it, and by blessing the cup of wine and sharing it; finally, by sending them out to share the good news. That's about as full, complete and clear a picture of the Mass as you are ever going to get.

So once again, my friends, here we are, gathered on the Lord's Day, not simply, as we say, to go to Mass. We gather on the Lord's Day to meet Jesus again. The only difference between us and those two disciples of Jesus at Emmaus is that Jesus should be no stranger to us. We've had two thousand and more years to get acquainted with Jesus. The point to remember is that we need to put our mind to all this when we gather on the Lord's Day. It would be nice, wouldn't it, if we could say to one another as we were driving home after Mass: "Were not our hearts burning within us when He explained the Scriptures and broke bread with us?" Well, perhaps we are not at that point of "burning hearts" yet, but it's something to be hoped for, isn't it? It's all about recognizing Jesus.

The Scriptures:
Acts 2:14, 22-23; 1 Peter 1:17-21; Luke 24:13-35

Year B

A FEW DAYS AGO I WAS sitting in our library here at the house paging through a history of the opening of the "West." The text, along with old black and white photographs described the tough and gritty lives of the settlers. Folks were standing outside their sod houses in their "Sunday best," people at country fairs, people having frontier fun, farmers turning over the sod.

One chapter, however, graphically describes the common method of capital punishment in those times—death by hanging. Some of the victims were obviously "gun-slingers," stagecoach robbers, and outlaws of various sorts. Several other photos, however, showed the hanging of several Negro runaway slaves. Obviously, this punishment was common practice in pre-Civil War days in order to deter others from doing the same.

But get this. What astonished me was the crowd of people witnessing the "event." This could have been a Sunday afternoon outing. Some (including many children) sat on the grass having their picnic lunches, eagerly waiting the final moment of the drop. The people did not seem disturbed or embarrassed to be watching someone's death up close. They were not holding their hands over the eyes of their children. They were simply sitting around, waiting to see how a human being died—an act gross beyond belief.

Who were these people? They were ordinary folks who just had come to witness (remember that word), indeed witness, an "ordinary action." It was probably not even considered a violent act, just Sunday afternoon entertainment in an age when true entertainment was hard to come by.

So, who were they? They were witnesses, on-lookers. Mind you, however, these people did not witness to or stand against the indescribable violence. They did not rise up to object to it. No, rather I should imagine that they stood in agreement with it. These photos showed people who came to watch (witness), but they made no effort to "witness" against the death of a human person or even against the grossness of the entire event.

So, my point is that we ordinary human beings can either stand around and look at (witness) something without demonstrating any emotions or, in contrast, we can stand and witness our feelings about some particular act that we find unjust. The more honorable of the two, of course, is to witness our concern and our standing against an issue. I am saying all this because the word "witness" threads its way through many of the Scriptures during the Fifty Days of Easter.

There are numerous occasions, for instance, when the disciples of Jesus witnessed his suffering and death, but also occasions after the resurrection when they speak of seeing him, eating and drinking with him, hearing him refer to the Jewish Scriptures as predicting his future apostolate. So important were these events in Jesus' life for the early Church that it would be unthinkable for them not to say what they had witnessed. This experience was too important to be left behind without notice.

Think then what Christian life would be like today if those early Christians, who were apostles, disciples, and just ordinary folks, had decided that those events were just not important enough to be witnessed, remembered, and passed on. What would our faith look like if that had been the case? It is a rhetorical question, of course, because we know that these Christians did, indeed, pass on the stories of Jesus that form our faith today.

That leaves us with the most important question: If we claim to be Catholic, where is the witness to that? How do we stand after having witnessed the stories of Jesus' life in the gospels? Does any other person, Christian or non-Christian, have any sense that we have "been there," that we are witnesses to Christ? On the quality of Christian witness, Thomas Merton, the Cistercian monk, once said that the saints preach sermons by the way they walk, the way they stand, and the way they pick up things and hold them in their hands. Well, that sounds pretty easy; but, our body posture truly tells others a lot about ourselves. How do we stand…where do we stand—that's the question! Witnessing and standing for—are they not practically the same thing? Is that not right?

The Scriptures:
Acts 3:13-15, 17-19; 1 John 2:1-5; Luke 24:35-48

Year C

OF ALL THE WORDS IN HUMAN languages that engage our interests in different ways and for different reasons, the word "love" must surely stand in first place. In some sense it represents our deepest feelings toward another and, in another sense, it is used to cover almost any human emotion: Love my Lexus, love my Blackberry, love my black Labrador retriever, love my million dollar job. Somewhere in that list we may also casually say: "Oh yes, and I love my wife, love my husband, and love my kids. But, we all know down deep in our heart that we don't really love that Blackberry. We may be attached to it, and it may serve our purposes. It may make our life simpler, but if we say that we truly love that small black instrument, our values are a little askew. Love is a serious word. It conveys the sense that we would be willing to give up all else for the sake of the person or persons who have cast their lot in with us.

In a short blog that I do every two weeks for *The Catholic Anchor*, that respected Catholic news source for the folks in the Archdiocese of Anchorage, I wrote a short piece about Jazz. I "love" Jazz (see there!) and one particular artist, John Coltrane (of happy memory). His music is what some of the young adult set call "truly cool." I bring up his name because of his four-part creation entitled "A Love Supreme." It is truly a supreme piece of work. I have listened to it many times. And then, one day a friend of mine pointed out to me that "A Love Supreme" was a psalm expressing Coltrane's sorrow for his careless habits of life and as a praise piece to God for rescuing him from himself. I pulled up the words of the music on "Google" and found them truly beautiful, full of sadness and pathos, but of deep-spirited joy as well. I wanted to bring up Mr. Coltrane precisely because of the words in the song: "God's supreme love for us."

There is a similar story of love in the gospel for this Third Sunday in Easter season. It is that lovely conversation between Jesus and Peter that occurred a short while after Jesus' resurrection. Jesus had just provided Peter and his friends a fine seaside breakfast of grilled toast and fish. Then after the meal, Jesus casually asks Peter: "Peter, do you love me?" Three times he asks Peter the same question, an almost exact repetition of Peter's three-fold denial of his teacher shortly before Jesus' death. After the third question: "Do you love me?" Jesus adds: "Peter, feed my sheep," that is, "have care for this flock that has followed me."

Did Peter really understand the question? Did he know what Jesus meant by the word love? I suspect not, but years later it became clear to him that love meant going the distance, being willing to die for his teacher and the good news he taught. It is an instance of "A Love Supreme"—being willing to make the supreme sacrifice if called to it. I truly believe that this short conversation between Jesus and Peter is one of the most beautiful examples of love between two strong-willed men that I have ever read. I am surprised that it has not been set to music.

The lesson in all this, I believe, is that we are all called to "A Love Supreme"—a full dedication, not to precious things, but to precious people who have been given to us for "caretaking." In some sense we are all entrusted with the life of others. We all need some special responsibility in our lives, something that will give us joy, simply because we are entrusted to do great tasks for God and for those who have cast their lot in with us for a lifetime. Believe me, it will eventually turn into "A Joy Supreme."

The Scriptures:
Acts 5:27-32, 40-41;
Revelation 5:11-14; John 21:1-19

20

Fourth Sunday of Easter

†

Year A

POLITICS HAS ALWAYS interested me, not in the sense that I want to be any elected official, but rather because the motivations of those who run for office seem so mysterious. Why anyone would want to run for the office of President of the United States, for instance, puzzles me. Either the candidate must have a large ego and loves being a power broker, or he is simply a masochist and doesn't mind being lampooned with cartoons in national magazines for the next four or eight years. Let's face it—politics is messy business. Large bodies of people are basically ungovernable and uncontrollable. Who would want to spend a large part of his or her life fighting political battles?

Realistically, of course, somebody has to do it, for whatever motivation. I would like to think that at least some politicians have a high motivation for running for office, despite its burdens. There must be some politicians out there who sincerely believe that they can make the world a better place and are willing to take the flack that goes with the office. Some (many I hope) are sincerely concerned for the welfare of their brothers and sisters, who are their constituency. I hope this does not prove to be a naïve hope. If it is, then our world is in deeper trouble than I already think it is.

Despite the bad reputation that the world of politics often has because of the individuals who use their office for their own ends, there is still something gratifying about being able to say that we have done something to make the world a better place. We have brought order out of chaos and the poor and the underprivileged have been served. Leadership, if chosen for a high motive, is a noble goal. Given the complexity of human communities, of course, leadership is an absolute necessity. Fortunately, there always seems to be some individual or individuals who rise to the top and pledge to do their best for the commonweal. Nonetheless, high motivation would seem to be required; otherwise chaos and harm will ensue.

Perhaps not many politicians think about their motivation, but if they were to do so, I would suggest that they think about being shepherds. I know that is not a very acceptable term today, because most folks in the community do not like to think of themselves as aimless sheep or people who need someone else to run their lives for them. Nonetheless, shepherding is an ancient and honorable profession. Although in our time that occupation is limited to a comparatively few individuals, the shepherd's task has a wider implication as a metaphor for anything that involves caring for someone or for many.

Whether we reflect on it or not, there are many natural shepherds among us: parents, teachers, social workers, political leaders, spiritual directors, bishops and pastors—popes even! Each one of these shepherds needs to be concerned about a different flock, but ultimately their task is to make sure that good order prevails and that people are served in whatever manner is important to them. In short, shepherding is an intimate part of life in the world. Without someone at the helm, life becomes unlivable.

It is not unlikely then that Jesus should have chosen the shepherd as a model for the vocation to which he felt attracted. When you re-read the gospel of today, for instance, you get the sense that Jesus did not have much patience with the spiritual leadership of his time. Those whose task it was to do this very thing were not caring for people. Indeed, he uses some pretty tough language for those entrusted with Temple or Synagogue leadership. He calls them "thieves and robbers." I'm sure that is a reference to the Temple taxes that the poor had to pay for simple sacrifices. He also calls them "strangers," because no one in the flock is listening to them.

So, what then is Jesus' model for leadership? What is a model that will fit our times, whether spiritual or secular? The metaphor Jesus uses best is this: "The shepherd walks ahead of the sheep; they hear his voice and follow him." Walking ahead obviously refers to good leadership. People, who look for leadership, look ahead not behind. Natural leaders are consistently "out front" of the flock, always thinking ahead, always looking for ways to make sure everyone is on the same page. Anyone who wants to be a leader needs to take charge and not wait for someone else to take responsibility. Responsibility goes with the job.

Another implication in Jesus' reference to being a leader is trust: Unless the people you lead have implicit trust in you and your leadership, you will never be successful. A third implication in Jesus' model of shepherd is respect. If you have no respect for those who look to you for leadership, if you are using people for your own ends, you will eventually fail. People will see through that motivation very quickly.

And finally what seems implied in Jesus' model is dedication. If you don't want to work hard, if you don't want to spend long hours figuring out what your people need most, you will not be fulfilling your task and responsibility.

In the end, of course, we would need to say that being a shepherd or a leader has many gratifying moments. If only one person on a given day feels that his or her life has been made better because of your efforts, then you should feel good about that. Your shepherding has been a model of God's grace. Hey, maybe that would be a good motive to run for office in the next election. Think of the good you could do.

The Scriptures:
Acts 2:14, 36-41; 1 Peter 2:20-25; John 10:1-10

Year B

A WHILE BACK A POPULAR MOVIE made the rounds of theaters around the country, receiving a considerable number of positive reviews in Catholic and secular magazines. It was also a big winner at the Academy Awards ceremonies. The name: *Brokeback Mountain*—a catchy name. Part of the reason for its popularity is the subject matter itself. It tells the tale of two out-of-work cowboys, who accidentally meet while seeking jobs herding sheep high in the mountains of Wyoming. After beginning their work, they realize that they are developing a close attraction for each other. The gist of the plot, therefore, concerns the fact that they are gay, which also poses a conflict with each man's desire to be married and raise a family. In the end, the story turns into a modern tragedy. They realize that they need to terminate their relationship, but in the process their relationships with their own families also break apart and ends. Brokeback Lives.

I leave the issue of gay relationships to others better qualified than I to discuss. Nonetheless, the story illustrated for me the deep and sometimes conflicting human attractions that can complicate our lives and our convictions that we need to be faithful to our word and to those to whom we have committed our lives. The title of the film, therefore, is apt. All our human relationships have a tendency to be frail and sometimes to break up despite our best intentions.

The reason, however, I chose the image of *Brokeback Mountain* to introduce these words on this Fourth Sunday of Easter season is because of a sub-plot in the film. The two cowboys are hired to spend an entire summer by themselves high in the mountains caring for a large herd of sheep. They find themselves torn between living up to their contract to keep the sheep together and struggling with their growing attraction and affection for each other. In the process the sheep are, at least on one occasion, left to fend for themselves in the midst of a snowstorm while being exposed also to the threat of roving coyotes and bears.

For people who seldom see large herds of sheep in rural settings and the effort it takes to keep them together, this film can be an eye-opener. The two cowboys who suddenly become sheep-herders discover that this is a task that demands constant attention day and night by taking turns staying awake. In addition, the weather can make life miserable for both herders and sheep. The hours are long, the living conditions aesthetically beautiful but primitive, the pay minimal, separation from friends and relatives a given. All of which makes you ask why anyone would want to take on a job like this, to say nothing of making it a life career. The answer, of course, is dedication. You have to love sheep if you want to take on a job like this. Without dedication, you will be a very unhappy person. I'm not convinced that the cowboys in the film had this dedication, but in the ideal world of sheep herding, this motivation is what it would take.

Americans, of course, were not the first to discover sheep herding and its attendant un-pleasantries. The people of the Middle East have been engaged in sheep and goat herding for centuries. It is one of the mainstays of family life in that desert land. I'm sure it has never been a profitable career, but simply provided small families or clans with sufficient resources to live.

Jesus, of course, knew something about sheep and herding, although, I suspect he viewed it from a distance. Nothing in the gospels says that he wanted to take on this career. Nonetheless, Jesus had a great admiration for the men (women?) who did this kind of work, because of their dedication and their willingness to put their lives on the line for their sheep.

I can just imagine Jesus watching these herders from a distance and saying to himself: "Now, this is a model of the way everyone should be living. We all ought to learn a lesson from herders because they seem to have a personal interest in these animals that depend on them to keep them safe, provide food for them, get them back into the corral at night, guard the gate, and all the rest. And in the process, they get little in return except the 'gratitude' of the animals."

What I am saying is that Jesus was attentive to life around him. He was always finding examples in daily life that provided him metaphors for what he called the "Kingdom of God." Some examples were obviously more apt than others, but everything in the world provided Jesus with a story about God and our relation to God.

Several insights come to mind from Jesus' use of shepherding as a metaphor for life. First of all, there are people among us who are natural leaders. Consider people in the world of politics, education, business, law, and medicine. Consider parents too and people who have the responsibility of caring for others, particularly those who depend on them for responsible leadership. As we know, that ideal does not always work out in practice. But, even in a less-than-perfect world, leadership is an ideal that we could expect to be followed; it goes with the job. Of course, many people don't think of their role in life that way. It's often a responsibility they feel they deserve, and sometimes are even "paid" for. Hence, there is often little personal dedication to the ideals of their mission. That means, of course, that the rest of us need to "hold their feet to the fire" and demand that they live up to the responsibility which is inherent in the position they hold.

And then there are the rest of us. We aren't exactly helpless sheep, fortunately, but we are definitely a "flock." That is what the Catholic Church has been called for centuries—"the flock of Jesus Christ." We belong to one another, and we depend not only on our shepherds, but on one another as well. We are a "world-wide-web," as the communication industry insists; which means, of course, that as members of this body we call

"Christian" we are responsible for each other. We are literally shepherds and sheep at the same time, whether we believe it or not.

Anyway, it's nice that we have one Sunday in the Church year to remind us of all that. We call it Good Shepherd Sunday: Christ the shepherd, we the sheep. There's much to learn from that rich and simple metaphor.

The Scriptures:
Acts 4:8-12; 1 John 3:1-2; John 10:11-18

Year C

LET ME SHARE WITH YOU an odd piece of memorabilia about my life as a young Christian. In the last few years of the 19th century and into the early years of the 20th century there was an immense influx of farm folk from Europe—Russia, the Ukraine, Germany, and even the Scandinavian countries. They chose to settle in the Great Plains where rich farmland was readily available at minimum cost. And so it was that Swedes, Norwegians, Germans, Ukrainians, and a few Irish settled the rich lands of central North Dakota. Few became rich, but it was a way of life. It was among such folks that we, a German immigrant family, lived. Generally speaking, the relationships between the various ethnic groups were cordial and supportive.

In the matter of religious affiliation, however, there was a certain "clannishness." Rarely did our family attend another church. Our pastor forbade us even to attend non-Catholic weddings or funerals. From the pulpit our pastor made it clear that we were to stay in our own church. "Those folks don't belong to us," he said. We were obedient Catholics. Nonetheless, such restrictions seemed harsh to us, because in the secular realm everyone got along so well. As I remember those times, it is my sense that the inter-religious restrictions were meant for spiritual protectionism. Our pastors were frightened that if there were inter-marriages, it would mean a decrease in membership. After all, we were a small Catholic enclave.

After reading the Scriptures that retell the stories of the growth and progress of the early Church, it became clearer to me why our pastors, all in good intent, warned us to stay away from people who actually were our friends. The point is that one's religion has a tendency to bond us to one another. We are all of the same belief and practice. We all know "how to act in church." This means, of course, that we have learned the Creed, the meaning of the Eucharist, and the common prayers. Knowing all this gave one a sense of protection. Other Christians also had their customs, but they were not ours.

The liturgies that follow the great festival of Easter trace out for us how the early Christians gradually banded together under one creed and one form of worship. They were early on a small group, or several small groups, depending on where in the Middle East they lived. They discovered early on, with the help of Paul's preaching, that if they clung to one another, their faith would remain constant and reliable.

So, where did this sense of bonding originate? We read of it, of course, in Luke's Gospel where Jesus addresses his followers as his sheep and himself as their shepherd. If they will follow his Gospel, his good news, they will be safe from harm. It was from this assurance of Jesus that the leadership of the early church soon developed—apostles, teachers, prophets, preachers, healers, deacons, elders, et al.

One can still recognize the need for leadership in the Catholic Church today. Loyal Catholics know what it means to belong to one another, with the pope as our shepherd and our local pastors as caretakers. We may not always feel comfortable with hierarchical structures, but at least we know to whom we may go if we feel lost in this confusing secular world. It is often said that no matter where Catholics travel, they will feel at home if they worship in their own Church. This is not to say that non-Catholic churches are dangerous. It is simply that we know who our religious confreres are. They speak the same words of faith and know the same words of worship.

Happily, our relationship with non-Catholics and non-Christians is far more cordial and understanding now than in the times when I grew up. Like many others, I feel completely comfortable worshiping with other communities. Nonetheless, we know that Holy Apostles, Saint Matthew's, Saint Henry's, Saint Leo's, Saint Peter's and Saint Paul's parishes are still our personal and permanent home. If we go there, no one can turn us away. We are sheep of the Eternal Shepherd, members of one faith and one worship. Well, in sum, it just feels good meeting folks on the Lord's Day who think and believe as we do. If you go there, you will know what I mean.

The Scriptures:
Acts 13:14, 43-52; Revelation 7:9, 14-17; John 10:27-30

21

Fifth Sunday of Easter

†

Year A

IT HAS ALWAYS INTERESTED ME to notice, at least among Christians, how important a role their church plays in their daily lives. Whether folks attend Mass regularly or not, they will ordinarily defend themselves as Catholics who belong to this or that church. If you ask folks where they live, particularly on the East Coast or, say, in Louisiana, they will tell you: "I live in St. Monica's Parish" or "I live in St. Genevieve's." Perhaps they will tell you that this is their church because it is the place where they feel ethnically and spiritually comfortable, welcomed and at home. Of course, they will also support and defend that church because it's theirs. At least that is their conviction.

For as long as the Catholic Church has been in existence, it has identified itself with the culture of the times in which it exists. We speak, therefore, of the "Early Church," Jewish and Gentile. We hear a lot about the deep faith of the Church of the Middle Ages, or the more rich and flamboyant Church of the Renaissance, or today the Church of the Second Vatican

Council. In every case the Church is identified with people, with their culture, their language, their habits and customs. One might need to say that the only Church that truly exists is the one that we know here and now, at this moment, in this place on this planet.

Another interesting element about Church is the question: "Whose Church is it?" That may sound like a silly question because the Church doesn't belong to anyone (not even the Pope). If the Church belongs to anyone, it belongs to Jesus Christ, the Founder! But we have a lot of rather sorry history surrounding this very question. Whose Church is it? Who controls it; who is in charge? I can still remember as a kid the disputes over who was in charge of our Church of St. Henry. Was it the church trustees or the pastor? In one instance, the trustees were so powerful that they actually persuaded the bishop to have the pastor deposed and sent packing!

Just recently we have a story in the Catholic news of the situation of a Polish church in St. Louis. There has been a battle going on for several years between the parishioners and Archbishop Raymond Burke over who owns the church's financial assets. The folks say: "The church is ours; we built it with our money." The Archbishop says: "Sorry, I'm the boss; I call the shots." In fact, it got to the point where the bishop closed the church altogether and excommunicated some of the parish leaders. The parishioners, for their part, went out and got their own pastor, a Polish priest from another parish. The battle continues in a pretty scandalous situation. But it tells you that people love their church, and not even an archbishop is going to take it away from them. Of course, if someone tells

Fifth Sunday of Easter

you that it's not about the money—it's about the money! Jesus must be weeping.

In the Boston Archdiocese a similar situation is happening. The Archbishop closed a number of churches. In the case of the Church of St. Joan of Arc, the parishioners have occupied the church night and day for several months and refuse to leave.

Well, all of this tells you that over the centuries the Church has not existed in a vacuum. It always seems to take on the patterns of secular life, and that is not always a good model. A good question to ask is this: What was it like in the beginning? What was in the mind of Jesus and the early Christians when Christianity took root? Obviously, Jesus himself did not set up any organization. Within a few years those early disciples began to organize themselves into bodies called churches. Most of them were smaller than our normal parish today. Hence, the atmosphere was more intimate and close-knit.

Let me say that there is an answer to the question whose church it? Listen to the second reading from the First Letter of Peter, and let me warn you ahead of time that this is not the sort of language we use today. Nonetheless, it will tell you a lot about how those early Christians, our brothers and sisters, thought about themselves. Here is how the author of that letter to the Christians referred to them (let me paraphrase it): "My brothers and sisters, remember, Jesus Christ is our living cornerstone, precious in the sight of God. And you too are living stones. Therefore, you must build yourselves up on the cornerstone that is Christ. After all, you are a chosen race, a royal priesthood, a holy nation, a people set apart to praise the God who has called you out of darkness into his wonderful light."

My friends, that is one of the clearest descriptions of Church that I have ever heard. It tells us who we are, and how we are related to Christ and what our task in the world is all about. How different that is from the way we often think of Church today with all our organization, all our laws, all the competition that goes on over who makes decisions, who has the power, et cetera.

It occurs to me to say, therefore, that it wouldn't be a bad idea if every parish, every Christian community, were to gather once each year, aside from Mass, and discuss questions like this: What does this Christian community think about itself? What responsibility do we take for our Church? How do we think about our leaders, the bishop and the local pastor? Do we collaborate for the good of our parish or do we struggle for power? The answers to those questions might give the parish a clear idea of how it thinks of itself.

The point is, my friends, we just can't take our Church, our Christian community, for granted. We are all living stones, as the letter of Peter described. We are built on the cornerstone that is Christ. Whether all this will change a bishop's decision to close churches, I don't know. Whether it will help Christians understand their role as members of a parish, I have no idea. But one thing for sure, if only we could decide to use the model of those early Christians we just heard about, we would all be a happier Church and the question of *whose* church it is would never even raise its ugly head.

The Scriptures:
Acts 6:1-7; 1 Peter 2:4-9; John 14:1-12

Fifth Sunday of Easter

Year B

I have had a lovely little plant sitting near my living room window for at least the last five years. I don't even know the name of it, but I do know that it grows pretty much without my supervision. Thank God for that! A while back, however, it just seemed to be spreading out all over the place, so I decided to cut it back a little. Wouldn't you know it; within a couple weeks the ends of the branches I cut off began to produce more shoots. No luck! So, I just gave up. I said to myself: "Plants seem to do what they are created to do and I'm just getting in the way. So, I'll just let it grow and it will probably do fine without me." And it has.

But people who know anything about plant life and plant growth will tell you that a little tender care will make things grow even better than they do on their own. Culling or cutting is an ancient art or craft. Farmers have found that they can help the process of making plants grow by cutting them back and in the process they turn out to grow even better on their own. Don't ask me what the chemical process is all about. I'm a small-time farmer at best.

As in all practical human endeavors, there is always some meaning in things beyond what we already know from casual observation. So often we will say: "That reminds me of something." I notice that it turns out so often in the gospel that Jesus was a very astute observer of ordinary things and events around him. He often found meaning in those experiences, even though they may not have been very important to others.

Vine-growing and vineyard production have been a main

source of work and pleasure in many parts of the world for centuries. Vineyards are referred to as far back as the Book of Genesis. "Noah, a tiller of the soil, was the first to plant the vine." We also know, of course, that Noah also imbibed a bit too freely of the fruit of the vine and became inebriated—not the first or the last time for this outcome, of course. By the time of Jesus, wine growing and vineyard work was a normal daily routine. In order to make the vines grow and produce good wine, there was need to cut them back each year. The purpose of this process may have escaped the ordinary person, but not Jesus. He saw something in the growing of vines and vineyards that reminded him of his relationship to the little flock that had decided to follow him. Their relationship to him was obviously very important. He depended on them for support and they on him as well. So, he simply tried to make it clear to them that they were all in his great vision, very much part of him and of one another—like branches are part of the vine. I'm sure the disciples must have picked up on that immediately, having walked along the lanes where grapevines were growing and seeing farmers out with their cutting tools, culling back the branches.

Now, the point that always arises when we read the gospels is this: That's all very fine, of course, but how does it all fit today? How should we interpret all this in terms of how we understand ourselves as Christians in our age? How does it help us to understand our sense of Church today? Jesus was not simply talking to the people of his own day. That would make no sense. So, that puts the question into our own lap. We, as Christians, need to know. If Christ is the vine and we are the branches, what does that mean? How are we part of Christ? What does it mean to be "attached" to Christ?

The better question is this: What does it mean to be part of this church, not simply the Mystical Body of Christ, but this little community I belong to, the only church I really know anything about? I think what it means in part is for us to keep asking in every age, how can the Church, even the little community we call our parish church, how can that community say that it is joined to Christ? Is it doing the things that Christ did? Does it have the mind of Christ? That, it seems to me, is the best way of evaluating ourselves and asking whether we are an effective Church or not.

If Jesus were to ask our church for a little "progress report," what would we say? Would we be able to say: "We're still connected. We still are trying in our own little ways to do the things you did. We are still trying to pay attention to folks who come to us looking for compassion and understanding, and maybe for food and support too. That's what you did, isn't it Jesus? We are also trying to pay special attention to our 'little ones,' because they were special to you. In short, we are just trying to be your presence in the world, because we are the only link between you and the world that we live in each day." I think that's what we should be able to say if Jesus is the vine of which we are the branches, that is, if we truly believe that we are members of the Body of Christ.

Another question Jesus might ask us if he were doing a little "Progress Report" on us would be this question: "If you Christians consider yourselves branches of one vine, how are you getting along with each other? Is there unity among you? Are you all supporting each other?" I think Jesus could validly ask that sort of question, and we might not always have a favorable answer because so often there are differences between us. So often in the past we have gotten into our little private enclaves of liberals and conservatives, liturgists vs. justice advocates, and other little private "special interest groups."

My hunch is that Jesus, were he with us today, would be a bit depressed over the ways we so often disagree with each other and, indeed, even find unkind things to say about the positions others take on various issues.

Overall, that does not seem to fit the metaphor of the vine and the branches or Jesus' hope that we should all try to be one. If we are not bearing much fruit, perhaps we need to ask, where's the progress? Jesus seems to suggest that we should bear much fruit. Is Jesus' great hope for the Church in the world coming to anything?

We are doing many good things, of course, individually and as a Church, but an occasional "evaluation" or "progress report" is always good for us. Jesus had great hope for us, and he is obviously still with us. We can't very well get along without the vine, can we? Vine and branches is a great metaphor, even though we may know nothing about farming or the advantages of pruning branches. We have to learn to think beyond our confusion and come to the heart of what it means to be Church.

The Scriptures:
Acts 9:26-31; 1 John 3:18-24; John 15:1-8

Year C

My mother Cecelia died at an early age—in her forties as I recall. She was the mother of eight healthy, happy children; I happened to be the eldest. The most personal memory I have of dear Cecelia is a very short conversation shortly before she died. Lying in her hospital bed, she stretched out her thin, feeble hand to me and said: "Lee, I cannot take care of you kids any longer. You are our oldest; I want you to promise me that you will take care of your brothers and sisters when I am gone." I could hardly imagine what life would be like if she were gone, but, amidst some tears, I said: "Yes, Ma, I'll sure try." I had no idea how this promise would be kept (I was a high school freshman), but I was so proud that she would ask me. Those were the last words I remember her saying to me before she died. Without doubt, the last words of anyone who is dying are especially unforgettable. I am sure that those of you who are reading this will have lasting memories of your own father's or mother's last words. No doubt, they will also have special meaning for you. We all have personal feelings for those we love.

Now, this is a bit of a jump, but the gospel of John you have been hearing for the past several Sundays is a remembrance by Jesus' friends of his final words at the Last Supper, on the night before he died. (Don't ask me how the disciples could have remembered all those words!) They must have been important to the disciples to be remembered. Obviously, these men were not relatives of Jesus, but he called them his friends, his companions, the ones who had traveled with him and heard his words during all those previous months. At that Last Supper, Jesus made a rather strange remark. He called it a command: "I give you a commandment that you must love one another as I have loved you." Now, I suspect that most of us take that phrase as a pious saying that can only be understood in Hebrew, or could be said by Jesus because he is God. Rarely do people, even lovers, command their friend to love them. Even more rarely do men use such phrases regarding other men.

Let me suggest, however, that this commandment is not simply an emotional outburst by Jesus at a moment when he knew his end was near. It is a love that far outreaches human love. In some sense, Jesus was saying: "Friends, I call you friends because we have gone through hell together, you and I. During these months we have seen some astonishing things that have never been seen before. We are on the edge of something big. I have called it "God's Kingdom," the kingdom of God in this world. I mean for this work of ours to continue until the end of time. I warn you, though, there will be times when you may want to give it up and go back to fishing and money-changing or whatever. But until now you have cast your lot in with me to extend this ministry. So, I tell you, in the deepest sense, that you are loved. I have given you all that I have. Be well; fear not. I will be with you until the end of time. Remember you must love one another as brothers in ministry. If you do not, all that we have begun together will be for nothing." It is in this sense that I think Jesus spoke when he said that he loved his friends to the end.

All of this is rather difficult for us to understand, mainly because we seldom enter into a life-project with a friend except in the case of the sacrament of marriage. The project Jesus was beginning was meant to spread out to the ends of the earth. We know all of that today, of course. Some men like Paul and Barnabas (mentioned in the first reading) and hundreds of others did carry out Jesus' plan unto the ends of their lives. So, what is the implication of all this for the Christian of the twenty-first century? For those of us who claim the label Christian, Jesus has also given a commandment. It comes to us through the lives of millions of Christians who have gone before us, fought for the faith and given their lives so that it would not fail.

It has often occurred to me that Christians today do not have the same "tightness of faith" that the early Christians did. For the most part we do not need to fight for our faith like many Christians throughout the early centuries did. Oh, we go to Mass, we receive the sacraments, we keep the commandments. Isn't that enough to keep us Christian? That is the feeling among some Catholics and Christians. "We belong to the Church," they say, as many others who belong to the Knights of Columbus, the Optimists or the Elks; "we pay our dues and pray our prayers."

If we take the command of Jesus to his friends as a model for today's Christian, it seems clear that we are called to something more than "church on Sunday" and the sacraments when it is handy. The kingdom of Jesus demands more than that of us. The final point I believe is this: No matter in what age we live, if we are Christians it is assumed that we are friends of Jesus; and if we are friends, then that last command at the

Last Supper is addressed to us as well. All I can say is that it is nice to know that we have someone who has loved us for all these many years. Jesus is a man of his word—even in the twenty-first century.

The Scriptures:
Acts 14:21-27; Revelation 21:1-5; John 13:31-35

22

† Sixth Sunday of Easter

Year A

Although I never personally met her, one of my all-time favorite people was Dorothy Day. She died in 1980 and during her lifetime she had several careers—a journalist, a socialist, and a publisher of a monthly "penny paper" called *The Catholic Worker* (It still costs only a penny!). She was also a convert to the Catholic Church. She loved this adopted church so much that she had no fear of taking on even the Cardinal Archbishop of New York on issues of war and peace. Most especially she was known for founding Houses of Hospitality that welcomed any and all from the streets of large cities. She personally took on the responsibility of making the daily potato soup and bread, making up the beds, and sitting and talking to people as long as they needed someone to talk to.

Dorothy Day wrote a book, an autobiography, late in her life entitled *The Long Loneliness*. It was sort of a sad book because Dorothy had experienced a hard life—first married, then divorced, then living alone. But we learn from her autobiography that she found her greatest joy in being with others, with people of all classes of society. That motive was probably the reason she founded *The Catholic Worker* and the Houses of Hospitality. She loved people and needed people to fill up her life because she was basically a lonely person.

It has occurred to me many times that perhaps most of us are basically lonely people. We come into this world all alone, and we leave this world alone. But in the intervening years we long for and search for companionship. We marry, we join social groups or religious communities, and we make friends—often for life. All this tells me that we cannot bear to be alone.

Whoever was the author of the Book of Genesis surely had a deep understanding of human nature. He was convinced that God created woman, because it was not good for the man to be alone; so he created a helpmate. Then he added this: "That is why a man leaves his father and mother and joins himself to his wife and they become one body." One translation uses the word "cling"; the man "clings" to his wife because she is all he has. Without her he will be lonely for all of his life. I have always thought those lines contained a deep insight into our deepest longings. Is it any wonder then that we spend so much of our life searching for that one person who will fulfill our deepest desires? I often tell young people at their wedding that from this day forward they are meant to "cling to one another." It is what will give meaning to their lives.

Despite this normal human longing, however, we are still destined to spend much of our life alone. For example, occasionally I will walk back into church after Mass on a Sunday and look around. Not a soul is left in the pews. I say to myself: "An hour ago this place was packed with worshipers. They depended on me to celebrate the Eucharist; they waited for a word of encouragement in the homily. But now they have all gone their way and I am here alone (with Jesus!)."

Some years ago when I taught at a university, I would often join the drama students and take a minor role in some play. Sometimes when the production was over, I would walk back out on the stage and look around. Not a soul in the seats; everyone had gone home, and here I stood alone on the stage.

All this tells me that at many times in our lives we need to admit that we do stand alone. How must it be, then, for those who are sent to solitary confinement in prison? I would find that unbearable. As I read the gospels and the story of Jesus' life, I have the sense that he too must have often been lonely. True enough, he would choose to be off by himself in the desert or the mountains. But we also know that he longed for the companionship of his friends—Lazarus, Martha, and Mary. He "hung around" with the Twelve Apostles, with the Seventy-Two and with many disciples. He was truly at home with the crowds. We also know, of course, that on the last night of his life he depended on his friends to support him: "Could you not watch one hour with me?" he cried out.

Perhaps it is not so unlikely that he decided to establish a community of friends that would eventually become what we know as Church today. It seemed the most natural thing in the world to call together his friends and tell them that he would not leave them orphans. Even though he must eventually leave them and go his way, he would send them an Advocate, the Holy Spirit, who would continue to be with them forever. I have always thought of Church as a gathering of friends at worship. True enough, Mass often seems like a formality that we take part in all alone, but it does not have to be that way.

There ought to be a sense of companionship in the pews and in the relationship of the presider and the folks. If there is ever a situation where ideally Catholics should not need to feel alone, it would surely be in Church. That is one place where we definitely are one big family.

So, all these thoughts came to me as I looked through the liturgical calendar and noted that next Sunday we celebrate the feast of the Ascension of the Lord, which was Jesus' leave-taking. And following that we celebrate the feast of Pentecost, the day of the Lord's return in the Holy Spirit. All that tells me that we should never consider ourselves orphans. Jesus has never truly left us.

Perhaps Dorothy Day had it right. The best way to escape life's "Long Loneliness" is to find a community and to cling to it. When you think about that, it's probably the only option we have and not a bad one at that.

The Scriptures:
Acts 8:5-8, 14-17; 1 Peter 3:15-18; John 14:15-21

Year B

HERE IS A NICE LITTLE PIECE of useless knowledge that I'm sure you have been waiting to hear all your life. It is said that there are some three trillion references to love on the Internet. Don't ask me who said so. It may just be someone's guess. (Who cares?) Nonetheless, outside of the so-called secular world, one version of the Bible itself cites the word "love" more than eight-hundred times. Again, don't ask me who counted. In two of our scripture selections for this Sixth Sunday of Easter, love is mentioned eight times. In this case I counted them myself, if that means anything. However, if numbers do mean anything at all, and I think they do, then the word love must be important to the human race. Perhaps it's more than a word; perhaps it is even an intricate element of our human nature.

As a starter, if you read the selection from the First Letter of John in today's liturgy and the words of Jesus quoted in the Gospel, you will see immediately that the theme of these post-Easter liturgies is love. When I first read them, I said to myself that I wish they would define it for me or at least tell me in what context they are using the word. But, you see, they just throw the word out there and assume that we all know what they are talking about and that we all have the same definition for it. That creates frustration, at least for me, because it means that I have to search for the meaning for myself and hope I am not interpreting Jesus' use of the word wrongly.

At any rate, let me start this way. As I was sitting in the sun on our back patio, jotting down some notes to get started with this homily, I was listening to a beautiful song by Anne Murray on my Ipod. It is entitled: "Time, Don't Run Out on Me." So, I stopped for a moment and said: "Hey, maybe that's it; maybe we spend our whole life, from the first breath we take until two minutes before we die, longing for that one thing in life that will mean something to us, something I would describe as our heart's desire." And throughout our entire life, then, we struggle to realize that one thing, hoping that life and time will not run out on us.

Think about this. The tiniest baby longs for the mother's

breast. That's its ultimate desire. The five-year-old wants his own way. The teenager longs for the girl or boy who will be his heart's desire, at least for this week. The young man or woman goes to college, hoping to secure a six-figure job when he or she graduates. That's the heart's desire? They ultimately marry the one who will be their complement. Bernie Madoff and lots of others swindle many people out of their savings, imagining that this money could end up being their heart's desire. Now some of them are in prison—too bad.

Finally, we reach old age and we know that death is closer than we ever imagined it could be. There is nothing more to long for; and yet, is it not true that no one longs to die? As Zorba the Greek says in Kazantzakis' novel: "A man like me should live forever." Does not each one of us want to live forever or at least as long as we can, in case there is just one more possibility that could fulfill our heart's desire?

The interesting and mysterious point in all this is that none of us really and ultimately understands what we are searching for. We do not understand our heart's desire; hence we keep searching throughout life, moving from one false start to another. I have often wondered if any of us will ever die fully happy, fully satisfied and convinced that we have now realized our heart's desire.

You may say: What has all this to do with love? Well, this is no definitive answer, but love seems to be that element in human life that directs us to something that will satisfy us and will give us full happiness and ultimate gratification.

The huge dilemma, however, is this: The human soul is never satisfied. This temporary human object of my love will never be enough. The soul is always hungry for more, whatever "more" is. I don't know if there is any solution to this longing, but my sense is that if we can manage throughout our life to direct our longing to the other, to that other person or cause—somehow imagining that we can ultimately satisfy ourselves—perhaps that would be enough.

I think that is why Jesus is such a beautiful example of this love. In his whole life, all he said, all he did, all he died for was done for us and for the whole human race. He had no selfish, personal intent. He lived and died for us…the other. I am even confident enough to say that Jesus was probably the only person in world history who died happily. Hanging on the cross, he had finally found his heart's desire.

So then, weak as we humans are, distracted as we are by worldly desires, it might be well occasionally to ask ourselves whether this one achievement or this one moment in our personal history is what we are ultimately searching for and that which will provide fulfillment. My hunch is that we will probably go on wondering about all this until the Lord calls us to our final heart's desire, which his kingdom where love is all there is.

The Scriptures:
Acts 10:25-26, 34-35, 44-48; 1 John 4:7-10; John 15:9-17

Year C

I have long been convinced that there is something basically wrong with us. Now, I don't mean you folks individually sitting out there in the pews or even myself as an individual. I'm sure you are all good and well-meaning folks. You don't ordinarily get up in the morning deciding that you are going to get into a fight with the first person you meet. Seriously, however, when you reflect deeply on it, when you think about the history of the whole human race, you will have to admit that there is a very basic flaw or disease that afflicts us. The basic flaw, to my mind, is the fact that we can't get along with each other. We have had evidence of being at war with each other since the first human beings have existed on this planet.

Look at our own biblical history: The first story after the creation of the earth is the story of Adam and Eve who get into an argument over who's to blame for eating of the fruit of the tree of wisdom. Their first two sons get into an argument about whose product of the land, Cain's grain or Abel's sheep, is more pleasing to God. Cain doesn't receive God's blessing, so he kills Abel—all this over a blessing from God!

So, my friends this scenario of violence has been going on since the beginning. I hate to say it, but we seem to be a violent people. It starts in the playground of the grade school and proceeds to the highest levels of government and society throughout the world. I'm sure, if I asked you, you could provide for me examples immediately from your neighborhood, the morning paper, or from "Good Morning America." Much news is news because someone is in conflict with someone else. Someone assaults someone else and usually goes to jail.

I hate to bring all this to you on such a lovely spring day, but it is true. One of the most common traits of our humanity is the fact that we are in constant disagreement with one another. We do battle with each other. Now, believe me, I do not have an answer to this dilemma, except to say that human beings, all of us, have the tendency to protect our person, our identity, our reputation, our name, and our goods against all comers. There must be a certain pride in us that makes us so defensive and belligerent.

Why, for instance, are we fighting two wars in this decade? Why are there so many uprisings and wars among African people, Hispanic people and Anglo people? Doesn't it ever occur to people of any race that life could be so much more peaceful and productive if only we were able to get along with one another? Think of all the hundreds of wars that have been fought here and there and the millions of innocent people slaughtered in the process.

It would seem to me then that any intelligent person would have to admit that if we humans were obviously created to live on this planet and to enjoy its fruits in peace, this has hardly been the case. Now, I am not about to claim that I have an answer to world conflict. Smarter people than I have struggled with this and failed. But, inasmuch as I am a Christian and a Catholic, one would think that I should at least have some insights about the relations of Christian and Christian, Catholic and Catholic. All I can tell you, however, is that I have read the Scriptures and have found there abundant cause to believe that at least Christians have good reason to be able to live with one another peaceably.

Alas, this has not been the case. From its earliest days the followers of Jesus have argued and struggled with each other. Peter and Paul had their differences. The Eastern Byzantine Church and the Roman Church have been at odds for centuries. Today, if we choose to read any Catholic newspaper, we will find abundant evidence of Christians at "war" with one another. And, my friends, all that despite what Jesus has to say to us in the Gospel for this Sixth Sunday in Easter season. Here are his words: "Peace is my farewell to you, my peace is my gift to you; I do not give it to you as the world gives peace." There it is, my friends, some of Jesus' last words to his disciples and to the Church: "Peace is my gift to you." Now, of course, Jesus also left us other gifts, such as the Eucharist, the gift of forgiveness, et cetera. But peace is the only gift he explicitly said he was leaving us.

Now, the problem is this: Peace or any other gift is still a gift. It can't change the way we live or the way we communicate with one another. In other words, Jesus' gift of peace is a model for the way we could and should get along with each other. Jesus' gift can't make us be peaceful. Peace is our responsibility.

Perhaps one of our problems is that we always think that if there is a problem in the Church, the solution for it should come from the highest level in the Vatican or the local Pastoral Center. The fact is, however, that neither of these ministries has the power or the influence to make us be peaceful. Peace can only happen when folks at the middle and lower levels of the Church decide that it can be done. Indeed, peace can happen only if individuals like you or me decide that we will put our personal difference aside and talk to each other. Then perhaps Jesus' example of peacemaking will make its way up the ecclesiastical ladder where people in high places can learn from us.

The final point I would like to make, however, is this: It doesn't seem to me that there are very many issues in this world, especially in the Catholic Church, that are so important that we need to be at war over them. In fact, there is a good possibility that we can come to some understanding if we have the good sense to sit respectfully with each other and just listen. I'm sure that if Jesus thought peacemaking was meant to be more difficult than this, he would surely have told us how to do it. In the meantime, the ball is in our court.

The Scriptures:
Acts 15:1-2, 22-29;
Revelation 21:10-14, 22-23; John 14:23-29

23

Ascension of the Lord

†

Year A

I would never have called my father a liberal, at least in the context we use that term today. He was always a careful and conservative man. He managed to get his family through the Great Depression of the Thirties, which means, of course, that he managed his money carefully. I can remember receiving only two "major" gifts from my father as I was growing up. He bought me a wristwatch for my high-school graduation. And then, at the train station when I was headed off for basic training in the U.S. Army, he shook my hand and I found there a fifty-dollar bill! Now, mind you, fifty dollars was no small change in those days, but I remember him saying: "Here's a little something just in case you need it." Then he gave me a hug—something he rarely did. He was conservative, of course!

I learned something from my father on that day at the railroad station. He was ultimately a softhearted, sentimental person. He also knew that this was the last time I would be part of the family. It turned out to be true. I never returned home again for any long period of time. So, as I recall it, this was an important moment for my father. Difficult as it was for him, he managed to say goodbye, even with a few tears in his eyes. This recollection reminds me of the line from one of Shakespeare's plays (I think it was *Romeo and Juliet*): "Parting is such sweet sorrow." Well, I don't know how sweet parting is, but I think all of us would agree that parting is something we do not look forward to eagerly.

The problem is that, at this point in our life, many things will change; nothing will ever be quite the same again. We will be on our own, for good or ill. Perhaps we could honestly say that at a parting we are all a little scared, especially if this is the first time we have left our family. What if we flunk out of college? What if our first job turns out to be more than we can handle? Could we ever "go home again" without embarrassment? By the way, that phrase came from the title of a book by Thomas Wolfe—*You Can't Go Home Again*. It seems to be true. Once you leave the familiar confines of the place where you grew up, you will find that it is never the same even if you decide to go back. What is fundamentally different, of course, is you. You have changed in the meantime. So, if we do go home again, it will not be the same person who goes there.

I wanted to talk a little about leave-taking because that is what we are asked to think about today on the feast of the Ascension of the Lord. Perhaps the word we use to identify this day is in some sense deceptive because it implies a "going up," Jesus' going up to heaven and back to his Father. I have no doubt that at some point after Jesus' resurrection he did indeed leave his friends. Whether Jesus "went up" is a question. But for the early disciples "up" meant the place where God was.

This was their sense of cosmology and their sense of the world. If Jesus went anywhere, it had to be up.

But we can set cosmology aside and simply ask about the implications of Jesus' leaving. What is really clear is that Jesus in the last few years of his ministry developed a very close relationship with some very ordinary people, men and women, mostly working class folks. What is also clear is that he depended on them to help him fulfill his ministry. They were to be his trusted confidants. They traveled with him; they preached as best they could; they took the responsibility of sharing bread with people. In simplest words, they were a "band of brothers."

I can't help but think, therefore, that after Jesus' death and resurrection he must have come to the point where he needed to say goodbye to this band of brothers and sisters and that this must have given him a sense of sadness. After all, they had all gone through a lot together, some good times and some bad times. So, it is interesting to notice that on the day he "headed for home," Jesus wanted to make sure that his disciples would not be in complete despair over his going. He says to them: "Behold I am with you always, even until the end of the age."

He did not say here how he was to be with them, but, for sure, this was not to be the end of the great adventure. Jesus gives his friends a task to continue working on: "Go and make disciples of all nations, baptizing them in the name of the Father, the Son and the Holy Spirit." The logical question to ask, therefore, is this: What did Jesus expect would happen at "the end of the age," at a point when the last disciple had passed on? Was this to be the end of the great adventure of preaching the Kingdom of God? Well, I have to believe that Jesus was smart enough to know that at some point his disciples would not be able to carry on his work. So, the only conclusion I can come to is that Jesus meant for his work to be carried on to the end of every age, throughout all of history. That has to be the only sensible way to understand Jesus' work—namely, that it now belongs to us, to his Church, with the help of the Holy Spirit, to carry it forward.

Of course, this work is about more than baptizing. It's about all the ministries that we have learned to take upon ourselves as Catholic Christians: Lectors, Eucharistic ministers, catechists, visitors to the sick, comforters of the dying, et cetera. In short, there are pastoral leaders of all sorts available, depending on one's unique gifts.

So, in the end we must say that we do not know whether Jesus was sad that he had to "go home." Given what we do now know from history, we would have to say that he doesn't need to worry. We're trying our best to "keep things together." Sure, we've made some mistakes, but, after all, we're human. The Church is human, but we can still depend on Jesus to keep his word: "I will be with you until the end of the age."

The Scriptures:
Acts 1:1-11; Ephesians 1:17-23; Matthew 28:16-20

Year B

LET ME START RIGHT OFF by telling you that this feast of the Ascension of the Lord is a very difficult feast for me to understand. I've struggled with it for years, but I think that this year I may have solved my problem. First off, it starts with the word "up." Now, that is only a two-letter word, but a very puzzling word in itself. You might think that up is up, right? But listen to how it is often used. The sun comes up, we wake up, we wash up, we speak up, we work up an appetite, we lock up the house; we look up a word, we add up our accounts, someone tells us to lighten up if we have stirred up trouble. And now, in today's Gospel, Mark says that Jesus was taken up into the heavens to be seated at the right hand of God.

It was from that one word, used three times in today's Scriptures, that we derive the title of this splendid feast—the feast of the Ascension. So you see how I struggle with all this? But, let me insist immediately that I do believe Jesus Christ was taken up into the heavens. How he was taken up, I do not know. What does help, though, are some other words. Jesus returned to the Father. Jesus reigns with the Father. Jesus Christ sits at the right hand of the Father. So, that helps me not to have to imagine Jesus going up into the skies like a NASA spacecraft or an Atlas Booster. I think those analogies are much too simplistic to compare to Christ's sacred experience.

If I had my way, I would change the title of the feast from Ascension to "Homecoming," or "The Last Instruction," or "The Great Commissioning." That's what I would title it and for this reason. There are actually only three references to "going up" in the Scriptures for this feast, one in the Acts of the Apostles and two in the Gospel. The main body of the scripture text has to do with other things. In those last few hours when Jesus was with the disciples, he consoled them, he promised the Holy Spirit, he instructed them, he gave them spiritual powers, and he assigned certain ministries, et cetera. So, all those arrangements seem more important than wondering what "going up" means.

Ah, but there is one more important element in this story. Jesus gave certain tasks to the apostles before leaving. My sense is that those assignments were meant for the Church. In other words, the last thing Jesus did was to make sure that the Church would not fail. So, he empowered the apostles to teach, to preach, to baptize, and to heal after he had gone. Most importantly, however, he told them that they must be witnesses to all that he had said and done. Now, I am assuming, of course, that this witnessing that Jesus assigned the apostles was meant for us as well. In fact, Paul in the Letter to the Ephesians even says so. It was not meant to be a hierarchical gift only, but a gift of the Spirit for all the baptized, you and me, dedicated lay folks, clerics, religious—everybody. How else should the Church survive throughout history? We are a human Church with divine gifts. "Go into the whole world," Jesus says, "and preach the good news to all creation."

I'm sure I could go on, but my time is up, so I will wrap it up for now and simply shut up.

The Scriptures:
Acts 1:1-11; Ephesians 1:17-23; Mark 16:15-20

Year C

One of the most difficult things any of us has to do at a certain point in our life is to say "goodbye," perhaps only for a few years, but in other instances, even for a lifetime. Once we have established a bonding with someone, such as children with their aging parents or a trusted professor who has helped us through college, having to break those personal bonds is almost counter to our natural instincts. We rarely choose to be separated permanently from anyone. A death in the family, for that reason, is always a wrenching experience.

So it was too for Jesus' twelve best friends when he told them (perhaps in tears) that he was leaving them and returning to the Father (going to Heaven). In their case, it was doubtless a more heartbreaking experience inasmuch as their entire lives, their past and their future, were intimately tied up with this special person, Jesus of Nazareth. They had abandoned their life's careers, perhaps their families and friends, to follow this itinerant preacher who claimed intimacy with God.

These are the basic assumptions that provide the foundation for the liturgical feast we call "The Ascension of the Lord." He had been executed for public disturbance and later was experienced by the twelve apostles for a period of weeks. Now he breaks the news to them that he has completed his work and needs to return home.

So, the Church names this sad event, "The Ascension of the Lord," the going up into the heavens. In one sense, the event might be better termed the Lord's leave-taking, rather than his going up. Yet, the title, "Ascension," in Christian usage is entirely appropriate. This seems so, not because heaven is "up," but because we imagine it is up. In a sense we cannot imagine that at death we will go "down" into the hell of the damned, nor can we say that we will go "out." To go out implies infinity rather than a point in "place." All this may sound like philosophical nonsense, but in some sense, the word "up" in Hebrew-Christian history designates the place of God or the place of the gods. It also refers to the place of mystery. Even looking up into the skies gives one a sense of mystery, of infinitude and the place of the Holy One.

Historically, in Hebrew usage, God dwelt above the skies in the place of ultimate divinity. Earth, on the other hand, was the habitation of humankind. Below the earth was the place of punishment, hell. We have many instances in biblical literature where the Israelites, and other tribes as well, climbed hills, high places, or mountains to worship God (or their gods).

Spiritually too, we look up to God to offer praise. In the Eucharistic prayer we are invited to "lift up our hearts." We respond: "We lift them up to the Lord." It seems so natural to do this.

From a theological perspective, of course, Jesus does not need to go up. Going up simply signifies going home to the Father. And where is the Father? The Father, in a human sense, can only be up and above all that is earthly.

A final implication is that the Lord Jesus did need to leave and return to the place from which he came. In his own words, he makes it clear that he cannot remain here on earth any longer, otherwise the Holy Spirit cannot come and fulfill all that he (the Christ) had accomplished.

Along with this understanding is the implication that there was still much work to be done by the disciples and their successors, who are the Christians here on earth, you and I, and everyone who believes in the Lord Jesus Christ. So, then, if nothing else, looking up is a sign of faith. Wherever the Lord Jesus must be, that is where our attention should also be, that is, in the place where the work of salvation is still in the process of completion. I can imagine Jesus saying to the disciples: "I've finished my part of the work; now you must finish it up. I'm out-a-here!" So long!

The Scriptures:
Acts 1:1-11;
Hebrews 9:24-28, 10:19-23; Luke 24:46-53

24

Solemnity of Pentecost

†

YEAR A

THE STORY IS TOLD of a heated argument between Napoleon Bonaparte, at the height of his power, and a certain Roman Catholic cardinal: "Your eminence," Napoleon said, "Are you not aware that I have the power to destroy the Catholic Church?" The cardinal, the anecdote goes, responded ruefully: "Your majesty, the Catholic clergy have done our best to destroy the Church for the last 1800 years. We have not succeeded and neither will you." Whether this conversation actually took place is anyone's guess, but even a cursory look at Christian history will tell us that it could have. Despite its history of various heresies, controversies, schisms, scandalous lives of Renaissance popes, cardinals and bishops, dual papacies, sexual abuse of children by priests and religious leaders, despite all this, the Church of Jesus Christ, guided by God's Spirit, continues to live and even thrive. Perhaps we must also look to ourselves and ask: "What have I personally done to build or annihilate our church?"

When one reflects on the life and history of our Church, it

seems obvious that despite the many failures it has sustained, it remains strong and life giving. The only answer to this human anomaly is found in the three Scriptures (Acts, Corinthians, John), in that astonishing story of the descent of the Holy Spirit upon the early Christians. The community of Jesus' disciples had no idea what they should do, or even if there was a future for them. Should they welcome Gentile people into their Jewish ranks? How should they find the time to preach the good news and take care of domestic responsibilities, such as caring for the poor, for widows and orphans? All this was beginning to bring discord into the community until that incredible day when God's Spirit blew through their gathering and brought with it an insight into communal living that has never been extinguished. That movement of the Spirit endures until this very moment in history as a smoldering wick, always prepared to flame into action when the community itself shows the incentive to do the new, the original, the courageous, and the issue that best describes the present situation in the world.

It should be remarked too that the Spirit is not simply a doer of remarkable things. The incentives for new life in the Church come from within the members themselves—people with new ideas, wild suggestions, brave original proposals that will enhance the life of the Church. For reasons of space, I could not even begin to name the multitude of individuals, women and men, over the centuries who gave the Church new life just when it seemed as though it was failing for lack of nerve and fresh ideas.

The point is that the coming of the Holy Spirit was not meant as a one-time-only event in the Church's history. If the Spirit could move the earliest believers in Jesus to overcome their reluctance to solve the huge problem of welcoming non-Jewish converts, could not the contemporary Church find ways to solve its many community problems? It is evident, for instance, that there are deep divisions in the Church today between traditionalists who wish to reform the reform of the Second Vatican Council and those who claim that we have not even broken the ice for new and fresh possibilities flowing from that Council. Do the two sides need to alienate and condemn one another? Is there not room for dialogue, for reasonable conversation? In short, the Spirit promised by Jesus is not time-limited; it still remains among us to this day. All that is needed for the Church to continue growing is for Christians to stop bickering and begin listening to the Spirit who, by the way, has never left us. To say it in another way: the Spirit cannot move without us. The Spirit is not the Church. The Spirit is simply the moving force beneath or behind the Church, waiting to be called on to bring the Church into life when there are problems to be solved and issues to be settled. In short, the Spirit will not change the Church for the better unless we decide that we will cooperate with our own insights, visions, and the expectations of our dreams.

Once again, we need to get over the idea that the coming of the Holy Spirit was a one-time moment or event in Christian history. The Spirit still waits in every age to see whether or how modern Christians choose to solve their problems and how they will use their brains and good will to get at the issues that affect Christian living. I like to use the metaphor of the tiger lying in wait for prey, and when the right moment comes, it springs into action. So too it could be for each individual Christian living within the Church today. The answer to renewal is not to wait to go into action for the Spirit to make the first move—for example, an ecumenical council. All renewal is local just as all politics is local. All this means that the coming of the Holy Spirit is not simply historical; it is dynamic and always happening, provided that the Spirit can find Christians willing to take the risk of foreseeing the future and doing something about it—always with the Spirit's inspiration of course.

The Scriptures:
Acts 2:1-11; 1 Corinthians 12:3-7, 12-13; John 20:19-23

Year B

IT HAS OFTEN OCCURRED to me as I gaze out upon a Sunday assembly gathered for worship that they are surely an interesting variety of folks: Old and young, kids in arms, teenagers. Even more interesting is the variety of nationalities and languages gathered out there. We Catholics at Mass truly make up a human kaleidoscope. I am sure that if our grandparents or great-grandparents were to wander into a typical Catholic Church today, they would be more than astonished. They might even wonder what country they were in. The reason for this confusion would be that, in their own times, the Catholic congregations that they were part of were fairly homogeneous and mostly Anglo-European people. Not only that, but if they were of German descent, they probably attended "the German church," and if Irish, "the Irish church," if Polish, "the Polish church," et cetera. But there was one common physical trait common to all of them. They were, for the most part, all white. If there were any black folks among them, most likely they would unfortunately be sitting by themselves in the back or in the choir loft.

Now, if those grandparents were to come into a large, metropolitan church in New York City, Chicago, Los Angeles or, indeed, any moderately large city today, they would see people from Mexico, from Central America, from Polynesia, from Africa, and from many other parts of the world. They might be inclined to ask: "Hey, where did all these folks come from? We didn't know there were so many Catholics in other places around the world."

Well, astonishing as that grand variety of folks may seem, it is simply a natural phenomenon of culture and history. There have been movements of people throughout history, due mainly to the fact that they came searching for food and freedom. And, of course, they brought their religion, their faith, and, indeed, their priests with them. Their religious heritage was important to them.

For a time all these ethnic and religious groups "kept to themselves." It was simply a matter of maintaining their identity. So, they went to their own churches. In large cities there might have been as many as four churches on four corners of a city block. So, naturally, they were able to pray in their own language, follow their own devotions and customs, or simply find a certain comfort in identifying with their own "kind."

Now that era of protectionism is past and folks today simply gather in the nearest church geographically close to them, but they also bring with them their customs of the past. Consequently, we may have as many as a half-dozen different "ethnic" liturgies in a particular church on an average Sunday.

So, at the end of this great cycle, we find the old traditional white European enclave being absorbed into a variety of other colors, cultures and ethnicities.

Is this good or bad? It can't be bad, for sure, when people of the same faith gather to share not only whatever is sacred to them but also the symbols and customs that carry that faith into the community. For all those who are open to this variety, they must come away the richer for it. I am saying all this because it is a modern-day picture of what happened on that day we Catholics call Pentecost, when the wind and the fire of the Holy Spirit came down upon the apostles and people began hearing them speak in their own languages.

Jerusalem, as we know, has forever been a cross-cultural city. People from all over the Middle East have gathered there, whether for trade, for recreation, or for the expression of their religious faith. So, in the reading you just heard, there were people gathered in Jerusalem from fourteen different countries and ethnic backgrounds. I'm sure that would be a challenge for any liturgist in our day! How do you get all these folks together doing the same thing? Looking at all this background, it appears to me that the Spirit of God has been gathering people of different languages, backgrounds, ethnicities and religions since the beginning of human time (whenever that was).

The point is that when people want to pray together, there is no human difference that can keep them apart. They will ordinarily rise above it. It must be said, however, that it is not always a simple matter. In our own day, for instance, there are differences that are quasi-political that keep poking up their heads. Christians and Catholics in our time are taking up sides called Liberal or Conservative, Progressive and Traditional, Catholic or Evangelical. A well-known Catholic writer, Father Ronald Rolheiser, recently wrote in the *U.S. Catholic Magazine* an article entitled "Knock It Off!" Basically, he was saying that it is time for Catholics to stop hammering each other and to start learning more about each other. Again, it's Pentecost time, the time when we should be able to accept our differences of opinion without getting mad at each other, calling each other heretics.

The long and short of all this is to say that there is a unity and a beauty in diversity. The universe itself is the best example of it. God, obviously, had good sense when he created such a variety of differences. What a dull, uninteresting world and a dull human community it would be if we all thought the same, lived the same, spoke the same, looked the same, and felt the same. As a matter of fact, we should simply be doing what we were created to do. Let us live with variety and enjoy it. I can just hear God's Spirit saying: "Hey, folks, if that's a problem, too bad. That's the way I did it. Get used to it!"

The Scriptures:
Acts 2:1-11; 1 Corinthians 12:3-7, 12-13;
John 15:26-27, 16:12-15

YEAR C

A WHILE BACK, shortly before Holy Week, I noticed some figures in a Catholic magazine predicting the number of people who were preparing to come into the Church at Easter. The article predicted that we could expect something like one hundred fifty thousand people to be baptized or to become full members of the Church. One thousand thirty-three in the Archdiocese of Washington, D.C. alone were counted. Think of that! That's a pretty astonishing number. Practically every church, small and large in the U.S. and in the world, will be welcoming at least several new members into its ranks. I imagine most of us who have been Catholic since the day of our own baptism might say: "Well, that's not so astonishing; the Catholic Church has always been attractive to a certain small number of non-Catholics. People keep dribbling in from year to year."

But, let me tell you that this is truly astonishing when you compare it to the so-called "old days," when one or two individuals each year might come to the local pastor and ask for "lessons." One of the great accomplishments of the Second Vatican Council was to restore the "Rite of Christian Initiation of Adults" (RCIA), a year-long process whereby non-Christians or baptized non-Catholics would choose to sit in the presence of other Christians for a period of a year or more and explore the Gospels, listen to the stories and tell their own story in their journey of faith. So, this incorporation wasn't just a matter of someone sitting in the pastor's study, taking "lessons in being Catholic." It was a family experience of Christian congregations sharing their faith with other searchers and learners. But, you might say, what's so important about that? Well, first of all look at the numbers. The number of people coming into the Church since the beginnings of the RCIA has just exploded. Something really monumental is going on in the Church.

I would like to say, therefore, that I think all this has something to do with what we are celebrating today with the Feast of Pentecost. The coming of the Holy Spirit, you may say, is "what, and today?" Is the Holy Spirit still moving in our midst today? Well, we often imagine that the coming of the Holy Spirit at Pentecost was a once-and-for-all "event," something that happened to the Twelve Apostles and has since been forgotten, or at least has not had any visible impact on the life of the Church today. However, the reason I say that the "wind" of the Holy Spirit is still blowing among us today is because that is exactly what Christ promised. He said: "I will be with you all days, even until the end of the world." In John's gospel, Jesus also tells his disciples: "I shall ask the Father and he will give you another Advocate to be with you for ever, the Spirit of truth…The Holy Spirit whom the Father will send in my name will teach you everything." That leads me to say, therefore, that God's Holy Spirit must still be active in the world today. Jesus promised not to leave us orphans (those were his exact words). The question, however, is this: How do we know? How do we know that the "wind of the Holy Spirit" is still blowing today? We simply need to look around for evidence.

First of all, consider some not-so-good pieces of evidence. Despite all our bungling throughout Christian history, we still manage to stay alive. Think how Christians have treated Jews over the years. Think about the Catholic Inquisition, the torture and the jailing and killing of "heretics." Think about the threat to the freedom of conscience. Think of the way the Church has treated creative thinkers, philosophers, and scientists, such as Galileo and others. Think about the abuses that led to the Protestant Reformation—the selling of indulgences and the wars between Christian nations. Think even in our own time about what we have come to call the "Sexual Abuse Crisis," with priests sexually abusing youngsters and bishops covering it up. The Church obviously has not had such a great record of living by the words of Jesus. I could go on and on about this.

And yet, the Church still manages to stay alive. How so? I think it is by the guidance and the protection of the Holy Spirit. "I will not leave you orphans," Jesus promised. But, are there any good things in the history of our Church that we could point to and say: "This is pretty astonishing! It could only be the work of the Holy Spirit"? I would first of all point to good Pope John XXIII, who called the Second Vatican Council that literally changed the face of the Catholic Church as we know it today. Just think how the liturgy has changed people's lives. We pray the liturgy in our own tongue so that we could understand and respond. All this has literally changed our Christian lives for the better. I think that is partially the reason why so many people are attracted to the Church today. Or think about the many trips around the world that Pope John Paul II took, and the millions of people who celebrated Mass with him in open fields. I think that's pretty amazing. But, some will say: "Look how the number of vocations to the priesthood and religious life has been falling. Thousands of churches, large and small throughout the world have no priest with them to celebrate Eucharist. What about that?" I say perhaps that is also a sign that the Holy Spirit is moving among us, prodding the Church to think about new ways to look at priesthood and pastoral life. Today many Catholics say: "Be bold, think outside the box." Perhaps that is what the Holy Spirit is asking us to do, to think outside the box for a change, to think creatively, to take a chance. Perhaps the Holy Spirit is asking the Church to do something totally new with regard to the ordination of priests.

So, what else is happening in the Church that we could lay at the "feet" of the Holy Spirit? Think about the numbers of lay people who are taking responsibility for the life of the Church today. Before the Second Vatican Council this was unheard of. Nuns, brothers, priests, and bishops did everything. Today you will find both laymen and laywomen in some of the highest levels of Church governance and in all kinds of pastoral positions. Could it be the Holy Spirit calling the laity to take on their baptismal responsibility?

Finally, I think about the role that the Church has taken in matters of justice and peace today regarding care for the poor and the oppressed. Think, for instance, what "Catholic Charities USA" is doing around the world today to assist in tragedies like Hurricane Katrina and other disasters.

Well, for me, all this adds up to clear evidence that the Holy Spirit is indeed "blowing" in the Church and in the world today. There is no way we could have done all this alone. In the end the question we need to ask is always the personal one: Is there anything spiritually exciting or new happening in your life these days? If there is, you can bet it's probably God's Spirit "blowing in the wind."

The Scriptures:
Acts 2:1-11; 1 Corinthians 12:3-7, 12-13;
John 14:15-16, 23-26

25

Holy Trinity

†

AT HOLY CROSS HOUSE, the residence where I live with other Holy Cross priests, there also resides an Archbishop, Charles Schleck C.S.C., a quiet, gentle, and humble man, who for many years attended to affairs in a prestigious office in the Vatican. He is reluctant to speak much of his tasks in this office except to say that he made many trips to Africa in order to "straighten things out." What those "things" were, however, he would never reveal. This same gentle man, in earlier days, was a theology professor for many of us who presently reside here. Occasionally we will engage him about matters of the "old days," that is, about his style in the classroom. One day he smiled broadly when one of the men in the group suggested that in those days we may have learned much abstract theological disputation, but we did not come away experiencing the God of the Trinity, the "Theophany of Three." "Yes," he would say, "those were different days. I hope you have found God in other ways since then." We all nodded and said, "You bet."

That encounter came to mind when I consulted the Scriptures assigned for the Solemnity of the Trinity. The feast we celebrate today does not define the "God in Three," but suggests ways to experience mystery.

It has long been my contention that no matter what serious-minded people may call themselves (whether atheists, agnostics, searchers or believers), they ultimately will admit that they do experience the "Sacred" in some manner. For some, definitions may do, for others theological disputation, but for the rest of us, who are the greater part, we will say that our lives would be meaningless without the experience of a Sacred Presence in the world. Without this, nothing makes sense.

For centuries, of course, serious-minded individuals have struggled to make sense of their experience. Our Jewish ancestors in the faith consistently turned to metaphor or images. The author of the Book of Proverbs, for instance, encourages his readers to develop that innate quality that all human beings share. We desire to experience God in God's creation. Whatever is good, sacred, holy, deep, impenetrable, overwhelming, full of wisdom, this is of God and this is the God of mystery. Moreover, the Jews could only imagine God in anthropomorphic terms—Father, Parent, Creator. The early Christians (Jews mainly, but Gentiles too) could only imagine God communicating with us through a Divine Messenger, who was Jesus, the Son of the Father. Jesus, the One who called God Father, promised that he (the Christ) would send the Holy Spirit, the Wisdom of God, to make all things new.

In the year 325, the Roman Emperor Constantine called the bishops of the Greco-Roman world to a Council at Nicaea, which ultimately gave Christians a technical definition of the Trinity—three persons in one God. This definition quickly found its way into the Nicene Creed, which all of us recite

Holy Trinity

each Sunday, and into our catechisms, which we memorize and recite as children.

Two distinct ways of experiencing God emerge, both true and apt, yet incomplete. Each of us must interiorize one or both of these models into his or her own spirit. It is at that point in our human experience that God becomes unique and real to us individually and personally. Finally, it seems only natural for us to use our intellect to find the "meaning" of God. At the same time our feelings, senses, and emotions are also a sure way to experience God "up close." I'm sure, in any event, that God will understand—even if we do not.

Scriptures of
YEAR A:
Exodus 34:4-6, 8-9; 2 Corinthians 13:11-13; John 3:16-18

Scriptures of
YEAR B:
Deuteronomy 4:32-34, 39-40;
Romans 8:14-17; Matthew 28:16-20

Scriptures of
YEAR C:
Proverbs 8:22-31; Romans 5:1-5; John 16:12-15

26

Corpus Christi

†

MY BOYHOOD HOME WAS SITUATED in the lovely Souris River Valley of North Dakota. Ducks and geese could be seen everywhere during the summer migratory season. Among the waterfowl a few pelicans could also be seen, searching for fish in the marshes and among the cattails, or flying low and slow over the water. Even as a youngster I knew what pelicans looked like.

What puzzled me, however, was the large ceramic plaque of a pelican attached to the post of the communion rail of our Church of St. Henry. So, one day, before Mass, I said to my mother: "Ma, what's that pelican doing up there?" "I've always wondered that myself," she replied. Later on, I asked the nun in religion class the same question, and she said it had something to do with nourishment. That didn't help much. At any rate, I have always thought about that ceramic pelican on the Solemnity of the Body and Blood of Christ, the very feast we celebrate today. Since then, I have discovered that the image of the pelican plays an important part in Christian iconography and liturgy.

For those of you who have never heard the explanation, I will save you a trip to "Google." The symbolism is rooted in a pre-Christian legend that during a time of famine or drought, a mother pelican would wound herself in order to nourish her brood and stave off starvation. I rather doubt the historical veracity of that story, but when one thinks about it, blood does have many meanings and applications. First, blood is in fact the very source of life. Theologians would say, for instance, that blood is a salvation symbol. It saves life and gives life. We all know, of course, what a blood transfusion can do. There are also many other secular analogies regarding blood. Soldiers shed their blood for their country. In addition, we often hear the words "blood, sweat and tears" regarding someone who makes a great effort to accomplish something. In our scriptural catechesis we hear the long-used phrase, "Jesus shed his blood for the world." What could that possibly mean for Jews and Catholics and everybody else?

I have come to the understanding that this is more than an abstract theological statement. I believe that Jesus shed his blood on the cross as the last great act of his life. He hung on the cross with blood pouring from his wounds because of what he believed in, what he taught, and what he died for—namely, that all people love one another and do justice. In short, it is no small thing for a person to shed his blood for others. If one sheds one's blood, it must be for some very significant reason—a reason that will have impact on the human world. This is the way I perceive the power of Jesus shedding his blood for the world.

The logical question that follows is this: Are we expected to follow Jesus and be ready to shed our blood for others? Well, perhaps not physically, but if we reflect on Jesus' life, there are countless ways that we can imitate Christ's life by sacrificing ourselves for others. Each of us will know what that means in the context of our particular human circumstances. These actions may not draw blood, but, surely, they will cost us something. Now, if my dear mother were still among us, I would tell her that I finally got the ceramic pelican legend straight. I know that she might say: "Hey, what took you so long?"

Scriptures for
Year A:
Deuteronomy 8:2-3, 14-16;
1 Corinthians 10:16-17; John 6:51-58

Scriptures for
Year B:
Exodus 24:3-8; Hebrews 9:11-15; Mark 14:12-16, 22-26

Scriptures for
Year C:
Genesis 14:18-20; 1 Corinthians 11:23-26; Luke 9:11-17

27

Epilogue: The Church at Prayer

†

An Exploration into Catholic Worship
Based on the General Instruction of the Roman Missal

IT WOULD BE SAFE TO SAY that we Catholics must often appear odd to many people in the world around us, or at least different—not in the way we choose to dress or act in public, but rather in the way we worship. If our non-Catholic friends should choose to join us on the occasion of a funeral or wedding, they will inevitably ask: "What's all this getting up and down you do, these strange gestures and signs you make, these pictures you have hanging on the walls of your church?"

Good questions. Many of these folks, particularly those of a more fundamentalist background, are satisfied with functional simplicity in their church buildings and, indeed, even in the very style of their worship itself: A soft recliner seat, a good sound system, songs that are simple to sing, a rousing homily by the pastor, and Sunday morning will be a success. For those of us who are Catholic, however, the experience of worship is more complex, but satisfying nonetheless. There is seldom a dull moment at Mass, at least for those who know the meaning of the prayers, signs, and gestures that have been part of our worship for centuries.

Catholicism has been accused of many things in its long and sacred history. But one label it has consistently refused to accept from its inception is the title "Gnosticism," an ancient heresy that claimed that human life is imprisoned in a creation controlled by evil or sinister forces. In short, for Gnostics, earth and matter are evil; things of the spirit are good. Catholics, on the other hand, have always lovingly embraced and respected material things, and indeed the entire universe: water, air, light and darkness, the beauty of the heavens and the earth as well as all the works of human hands—bread and wine, oil and incense, the light of candles. We lift up our hands and hearts to the One who has created the very things we need to speak words of worship and prayer. As baptized and redeemed Christians, we stand erect at the proclamation of Jesus' words. All these material things, these signs, postures and gestures, are important to us, not in themselves, but because they are doors to the sacred. We realize, along with the apostle Paul, that as human beings we have no other access to God than through the things of Earth.

We are safe in saying all this, of course, because Jesus himself saw signs of God's spirit buried in earthly realities. He spoke eloquently of the lilies of the field and the birds of the air. When life became burdensome for him, he retreated with his friends and disciples into the silence of the mountains or the desert. Bread for him was a sign of God's nourishment, wine a sign of joy and celebration, water a sign of God's gift to quench our thirst for eternal life. Nothing escaped Jesus' notice. He had eyes to see and the understanding to comprehend all that was naturally sacred.

It has, therefore, been the task and indeed the joy of our Church over the course of many centuries to point out for us all those realities that help us lift up our hearts in prayer. In simplest terms, it is called "liturgy," a work of the people. However, there sometimes lurks a danger in our symbolic use of material things in liturgy. Because we repeat them so often, there is the tendency for us, as in many other human actions, "to do the right thing for the wrong reason." We become trapped in performing the action, while overlooking its meaning. The German poet and dramatist, Johann Wolfgang von Goethe, pointed this out to us in these lines:

> In every new situation
> we must start all over again,
> like children,
> to cultivate a passionate interest
> in things and events,
> and begin by taking delight in externals,
> until we have the good fortune
> to grasp the substance.

This must be our task as Catholics, therefore, never to be satisfied simply with externals, with signs of the sacred, but rather to let them lead us in our search for substance, and for the God who is the source of all our prayer, all our longing.

In the following articles we shall attempt to explore our Catholic worship, asking not only what we do but why we do it. Our resource shall be the *General Instruction of the Roman*

Missal, that ancient book of prayers and directions that has for centuries given us guidance in our efforts to worship the God who gives meaning to our prayer and is the very substance of all we say and do.

Gathered in Steadfast Faith: What We Do, Why We Do It

All of us, from time to time, find ourselves gathered in groups, large or small, to celebrate some event that is important to us as a community. In order for such events to flow smoothly and make it possible for all to participate fully both as individuals and as a group, we assume that there will need to be certain rules or directions that will help us participate as a body. Indeed, we are even willing to give up some of our individual habits and preferences for the good of all. Otherwise chaos may ensue. Our Catholic Church has a long history and much experience in gathering people together to celebrate liturgical events. Whether it is a small rural church with a congregation of five families, or a papal Mass accommodating thousands of people in the palazzo of St. Peter's in Rome, both assemblies will assume that there will be certain rubrics, or directions, to assist the faithful in their prayer responses, gestures, and postures so that they can truly say that their common faith is being expressed and that they are worshiping together as a family.

The rules that appear in our liturgical books are called rubrics. They are printed in red so as to set them apart from the prayers themselves. They are important inasmuch as they give the priest and the assembly directions for worship. Because liturgical worship, like other human experiences, is a living experience celebrated by living individuals, we will often find that it will change from time to time, adjusting to the times and cultural circumstances in which we live. The "Vatican Congregation of Divine Worship and the Sacraments" is the Office that guides the church in its celebration of the Mass and sacraments. You may ask, "Where can we find those rules and guidelines for Catholic worship?" You will find them in a special section in the front of the Sacramentary, or prayer book, that the priest uses at the altar at Mass. It is called the *General Instruction of the Roman Missal* (GIRM). It is also published separately in book form and can be purchased from the United States Conference of Catholic Bishops in Washington, D.C. The General Instruction was first published shortly after the Second Vatican Council. It has been modified several times since the council. The latest edition was published in 2002.

Because our church believes in adapting the liturgy to various cultures "for the life of the world," bishops of each country have been given permission by the Holy See to adapt certain parts of the General Instruction so that the celebration of Mass may be more fittingly celebrated in each land. The bishops of the United States, therefore, have adapted some of these general norms to fit the needs of the Catholic Church in our own country.

Why are these explanations on the General Instruction important? Those of us who are middle-aged and older will remember the sudden changes in the liturgy shortly after the Second Vatican Council. Many Catholics, indeed, many priests and a few bishops, did not understand what changes were coming and why they were being made. There was very little explanation about why all this was being done and why we were being asked to "change gears" so radically. The order of our worship and the depth of our faith will depend upon a clear understanding of what we are asked to do and why.

The Search for Community

Many of us who are middle-aged or older will remember what Mass was like before the Second Vatican Council. We came to Mass not only out of a sense of obligation, but because it was the time each week that was set aside for "God and me." Although we came in large numbers, we came and left as individuals. The liturgy was our private devotion, our private prayer. Each person was on his own: Some prayed the rosary, others said devotional prayers or tried to follow the Mass in Latin using the "Peoples' Mass Book." Many simply prayed silently from the heart. Most Catholics, being people of deep faith, tried to get along as best they could alone, not knowing what the priest was saying or doing up in the sanctuary. A word we often used to describe our Sunday worship experience was "attend." We attended Mass, but we seldom prayed together as a community.

This is not the way the Christians of the early church worshiped. From the letters of St. Paul, for instance, we learn that he often needed to remind them that when they came together on the Lord's Day they came not only to celebrate the Lord's Eucharist, but also to share their household food, making sure that no one went hungry. They truly needed to remember that in all things they were community. Over the centuries, however, for many reasons, the Mass became less and less the celebration of all God's people under the leadership of the bishop or priest. The Mass became instead the prayer of the clergy.

Since the language of the Mass continued to be in Latin long after Latin ceased to be the tongue of the people, Mass became more and more unintelligible. No wonder people gradually developed their own prayers and devotions at Mass. They knew no other way to participate except to pray while the priest "said Mass." This great chasm between the prayer of the priest and the prayers of the people became more and more evident over the years. Hence, one of the first efforts of the bishops at the Second Vatican Council (Oct. 11, 1962, through Dec. 8, 1965) was to make the sacred liturgy more accessible to the people.

Indeed, the first document the bishops produced at the council was entitled "Constitution on the Sacred Liturgy" (*Sacrosanctum Concilium*). Several important sentences in that document have since become enshrined in Catholic thought and worship: "Mother Church earnestly desires that all the faithful should be led to that fully conscious and active participation in liturgical celebrations which is demanded by the very nature of the liturgy. Such participation by the Christian people as 'a chosen race, a royal priesthood, a holy nation, a redeemed people,' is their right and duty by reason of their baptism. In the restoration and promotion of the sacred liturgy, this full and active participation by all the people is the aim to be considered before all else; for it is the primary and indispensable source from which the faithful are to derive the true Christian spirit."

If this is our "liturgical constitution," our mandate as Christians, how are we expected to worship actively when we gather on the Lord's Day? We are asked to use all those human gifts that we normally use in daily life:

> The community stands at the entrance procession to welcome Christ in our midst.
>
> We are seated, keeping reflective silence, as the words of Scripture are proclaimed.
>
> We pray and sing together in dialogue with the priest.
>
> We kneel as a sign of penitence.
>
> We stand as baptized Christians to acclaim the words of Christ in the Gospel.
>
> We walk in procession as we bring our gifts of bread and wine to the altar or as we come once again to the table to receive those sacred gifts.

All of these words, these postures, these actions are done not simply for the sake of uniformity or good order. Rather, we do them together as a sign that the liturgy itself has the power to bond and bind us together as a community of Christians, acknowledging Christ's presence in our midst.

The fact that we all may be together in the same building each Sunday does not automatically make us a Christian community. It is rather our recognition of one another as brothers and sisters of Christ, praying as a body, that makes the liturgy that "primary and indispensable source from which we derive the true Christian spirit." In short, we desperately need one another when we gather on the Lord's Day.

Christ Is Present for Mass—Bells Are Unneeded

One of the memories that "pre-Vatican II" Catholics have of the Mass as it was then celebrated was the anticipation of the sound of bells or chimes at the time of the consecration. We knew immediately that we could look up at that time and adore the presence of Christ in the Host and Precious Blood as they were being held aloft by the priest (sometimes for a lengthy space of time). For most Catholic folks, this was the prime moment in the Mass, the time when Catholics could be one with their Lord. To be distracted or to miss the sound of the bells was tantamount to missing Mass. It never occurred to us then (how could it?) that there might be other ways that Christ was present when we gathered for liturgy.

When the bishops met for the Second Vatican Council, one of the key principles they put forth regarding the liturgy was that Christ is present in the liturgy in four unique ways:

1. In the Eucharist broken and shared
2. In the person of the minister
3. In the word of God
4. In the assembled people of God

In the *General Instruction of the Roman Missal* (GIRM), the directions that guide priests and other liturgical ministers in celebrating the Mass, the first presence of Christ mentioned is that of his presence in the assembled people of God (No. 27). Christ is present when the assembly is gathered in his name. This is precisely what Christ promised: "Where two or three are gathered together in my name, there am I in the midst of them" (Mt 18:20). Therefore, each time we come together to celebrate the liturgy, singing and praying, Christ is present in and with us.

The second way in which Christ is with us in the liturgy is in the person of the minister. Christ is present to us in the priest who is called the presider or priest-celebrant of the liturgical assembly. He leads the community in prayer and helps us to understand the words and actions of the liturgy. When he does so, he also acts in the person of Christ, on our behalf. He does this especially by the way he acts and speaks with dignity, reverence, and humility so that the living presence of Christ is conveyed in and through him.

The third form of Christ's four-fold presence in any liturgy we celebrate is in the Word of God. No matter whether we participate in a Mass, the other sacraments, or the Liturgy of the Hours, we always hear the Word of God proclaimed in Scripture. Whether that reading is from the Old or New Testament, Christ is present in the Word. In fact, at the beginning of John's Gospel, we hear that Christ is the Word of God. He is God speaking to us. And so each time we hear God's Word from a prophet, a psalm, a Gospel, a letter, or any other Scripture passage, Christ is there for us and with us.

The fourth way Christ is present to us in the liturgy is in what the church calls the "Eucharistic species." This is the preeminent presence of Christ. Christ is especially present in the bread and wine that become the Body and Blood of Christ. What looks likes bread and wine has truly become Christ's Body and Blood by the taking, blessing, breaking and sharing of the presider and the gathered assembly and by the grace of God.

Was it not in the "breaking of the bread" that the disciples at Emmaus recognized Jesus present with them?

What this should mean to Catholics gathered for Mass, therefore, is that they need not wait until the bells ring at the consecration to realize that Christ is present. Indeed, the very moment we gather with one another in the house of the church, Christ is already present. When we hear and respond to God's word, when the presider leads us and invites us to pray together, Christ becomes more and more visible and discernible to us.

All this takes us back again to the importance of signs and symbols. As human beings in our search for God, we need all the help we can get!

Processions Are a Ritual Expression of Ourselves

Most Catholics think that the liturgy begins with the sign of the cross. However, liturgy begins the moment we arrive in the church parking lot. Indeed, there is wisdom in that expectation, at least for the person who has given some thought beforehand to the Scriptures assigned for the liturgy of the day. Even from the viewpoint of time and distance, Mass does begin when we begin making our way, mentally, emotionally and physically, to the place of worship. One might say that there are grand neighborhood processions that begin on Sunday mornings as Catholics from all directions drive or walk from their homes and converge on the parking lots of the church and from there make their way into the sacred precincts. Getting there is ultimately more than covering some ground between home and church. In the words of the psalms, it is "going up to the house of the Lord." Spiritually speaking, therefore, walking or traveling is a sacred experience.

It has obviously been done for centuries. People find the need to go from their homes, their domestic church, to the place where the entire community, the assembly, gathers for prayer and worship. We call such movement processing, making one's way from one place to another for a sacred purpose.

Muslims have a similar concept they call "the Hajj," the journey to Mecca. Jewish people make their way to the holy Western Wall of the temple to pray. Christians also have been processing to their sacred shrines for centuries: Compostela, Fatima, or Lisieux, for example. There is obviously something that occurs at those sacred places that the Christian cannot experience at home. It is worth the time and effort to "get there."

Theologically and liturgically speaking, processions are a bodily or ritual expression of who we are and what we are about. We are pilgrims on a journey, a journey to God's kingdom. Indeed, all life—from birth to death, from baptism to last anointing—is such a journey.

For Roman Catholics there are also certain special processions within the sacred liturgy, which are models or paradigms of the great pilgrimage we call life. First, we make our way as a community into the house of the Lord. It is called the entrance procession. The ministers of the liturgy also make this procession to introduce the Mass, moving from the entrance of the church into the sanctuary to the accompaniment of song.

The Book of the Gospels is carried in a place of honor in the procession as though to say Christ comes among his people. Later, at the time of the proclamation of the Gospel, the deacon or priest, accompanied by acolytes and incense bearer, process with the Book of the Gospels to the ambo from which the Gospel is proclaimed.

Several other processions also occur at Mass: The people's

offerings are brought to the altar to be prepared and set apart for Eucharist. The assembly approaches the altar at Communion time to partake of the sacred gifts they offered earlier. At the conclusion of Mass, the entire assembly makes its way out of the church in a sending-forth procession (hopefully not in a mass exodus!) and people return once again to their homes, which is the domestic church.

Lastly, we Catholics also have a long tradition of special processions: On Palm Sunday we commemorate Jesus' triumphant entry into Jerusalem. We process to adore the cross on Good Friday. On the feast of Corpus Christi we process in adoration of the Lord's body and blood.

Finally, we process as we celebrate sacraments: baptisms, weddings, and funerals. Processions are not just a way to get people or ministers from here to there. Truly, they are a ritual expression of who we are—God's pilgrim people on life's journey to the kingdom.

Time-Tested Practices Dictate Postures and Gestures

Much to our embarrassment, our friends can often tell us how we are feeling before we say a word. Our bodies, particularly our facial expressions, speak volumes for us. Body language it's called. We cannot prevent it; we act the way we feel, and of course we all know the wide range of our emotions. We also know that the positions of our body assist us in accomplishing certain things that we may plan to do. When we wish to take a nap, for instance, we lie down. If something important is about to be said in a meeting, we sit erect and keep alert. If an important person comes into our midst, we stand up in recognition. If we want to relax to watch a sports event, we sit in a comfortable position.

Bodily positions can help us participate in the human activity we have chosen.

For Catholics, all this is particularly important because we are a people who pray not only with our lips and our voices but also with our bodies. The position that we take enhances what we reflect on with our mind and speak with our lips. For that reason our church has wisely integrated certain bodily positions into our prayer life.

Postures

Sitting is a posture of attentive listening and meditation. For that reason, we sit for the Scripture readings before the Gospel. We remain seated as the gifts of bread and wine are being collected, prepared and set apart for Eucharist. After receiving Holy Communion and when the Eucharist has been replaced in the tabernacle, we sit for some moments of quiet thanksgiving.

Standing is a posture which identifies us most uniquely as human persons. Standing is also a posture of respect, honor and reverence. From the days of the early church standing has been understood as the posture of those who are risen with Christ.

So the *General Instruction of the Roman Missal* calls the assembly to stand for the proclamation of the Gospel, for the reception of Holy Communion, and for many of the prayers addressed to God.

Kneeling, from the earliest days of the church, has signified penance; indeed, so much so that believers were forbidden to kneel on Sundays and during the Easter Season when the spirit of the liturgy should be joyful and thankful. In more recent times, kneeling has also become a posture of adoration. It is for this reason that the U.S. bishops have adapted the *General Instruction* to call for the posture of kneeling for the entire Eucharistic prayer. As the *General Instruction* points out, "A common posture ... is a sign of unity of the members of the Christian community gathered for the Sacred Liturgy: It both expresses and fosters the intention and spiritual attitude of the participants" (No. 42).

Gestures

It is sometimes said that we Catholics, who have the longest tradition of using certain gestures in our liturgy, often appear reluctant, even stuffy, in their use. If one wishes to experience religious gestures in their most exuberant form, we need only attend a group of fundamentalist Christians at worship, or a community of African-American Baptists. These folks have no reluctance in using hands and arms, and indeed their entire bodies, to pray. Nonetheless, reluctant as we often seem in the use of our sacred gestures, there are several such gestures that have been our practice for centuries and that speak volumes about our prayer.

The *sign of the cross*, which begins and ends every liturgy, recalls the one who suffered and died for us on the cross. In fact, the sign of the cross begins and ends all we do as Catholics—from the cross we receive at baptism to the cross that is made over our body at death.

Many Christians spontaneously *lift their hands* in prayer when so invited or at the Lord's Prayer. As a sign of respect for the words of Christ when they are publicly proclaimed at the Gospel, we *sign ourselves on the forehead, lips and breast.*

We *bow* at the words of the Incarnation during the creed and before we receive the Body and Blood of Christ. We bow to the altar, the sign of Christ present, when we enter or leave the church. If the tabernacle is located in the sanctuary, we *genuflect* in reverence to the bodily presence of Christ.

In short, we may not seem very emotionally demonstrative in our external gestures, because we are recipients of an ancient Roman tradition that observes moderation and brevity in all things sacred. We know the meaning of the old saying, "Less is more."

Everyone Should Feel Welcome at Catholic Mass

Every community that gathers for an event of local interest, secular or sacred, will obviously be a blend of people, differentiated in many ways: age, culture, personal interest, physical and mental capacities, etc. One thing's for sure: We all do not fit neatly into the same space in the same way although the assumption often is that we do or should! Unfortunately, as a church, a community of Christians, we have often assumed that everyone who comes to church will fit equally into the same sacred space and will have normal and equal access to all the sacred gifts that are offered there. That is not always the case, of course, and we are embarrassed to say that we "never noticed."

Many people who join the community for Sunday liturgy

come with special needs. They come to pray and worship, but they need special and loving attention particularly in terms of access and physical space. The seating arrangements in our churches do not always adapt themselves well for those who are elderly and infirm, for those who are physically or mentally disabled, or even for parents with children. Moreover, it must truthfully be said that even our rules for liturgy, which are meant to bond us into a community, often discriminate against those who are disadvantaged. Many people, for instance, find it difficult to stand for long periods of time. Others cannot kneel for parts of the liturgy. Many others need to be close to the sanctuary to be able to see and/or hear. Those who come in wheelchairs need access to Communion stations. Everyone needs a clear understanding of where the nearest exit is.

The ministry of hospitality, therefore, is becoming more and more a Christian demand in our churches. What is of utmost importance, of course, is a Christian community that has learned the rules of Christian etiquette—or better, Christian service in the model of Jesus. There should never be an occasion in our churches when anyone feels unnoticed or unwelcome. That would be the height of un-Christian behavior. As Christians, as God's people, we ought to be able to say: "Come as you are. There is room for everyone."

Mass Can Be Exhausting, and That Is a Good Thing!

Those of us who are old enough to remember our Church before the 1960s and before the Second Vatican Council may recall how we often thought about our Sunday morning experience. We referred to it as "going to Mass," much as we might say, "I'm going to the ball game," or, "I'm going to a movie," or, "I'm going to work." Our sense was that we were going to a church, to a place where something was going on—indeed, where something would be done for us, much like a performance in a theater. That often left Catholics with a sense of passivity, or even a feeling of apathy. There wasn't a lot we could do. The basic actions or responsibilities in the Mass were handled mainly by the priest, the acolytes (altar servers) and the choir. For many Catholics, therefore, the Sunday "obligation" was fulfilled by going to Mass, going to Communion and going home. Not a very exciting experience!

When the Catholic bishops of the world, gathered at the Second Vatican Council, began to think about the state of Catholic worship, their first concern was how to invest the participation of the Christian assembly in the action of the Mass. In the first document the bishops produced, "The Constitution on the Sacred Liturgy," they taught that "every liturgical celebration (Liturgy of the Eucharist, Liturgy of the Word, Liturgy of the Hours, and Sacraments) is an action of Christ together with his body, the Church. Therefore, the full, conscious, and active participation by all the people is the aim to be considered above all else, for it is the primary and indispensable source from which the faithful are to derive the true Christian spirit" (No. 7).

We Catholics may not have realized it then, but these were some rather explosive words. We had never been told that active participation at Mass was "the primary and indispensable source" of "the true Christian spirit." Now we know! It needs to be said, however, that we have been trying to get used to that mandate ever since the days of the council. It has not always been easy. Nonetheless, when one examines the structure of the Mass, there are some fundamental actions that belong by right to the Christian assembly.

First is the *gathering*—more than simply "getting into church and finding a pew." When we come together for liturgy we gather for a purpose. We come to worship our God and to establish communion with one another in spoken and sung prayer.

Second, we gather in order to *listen*. Indeed, that is what we do during the first part of the Mass, the Liturgy of the Word, which extends from the first reading through the prayers of intercession. But this listening is not passive. It is something we do. It takes effort and concentration to carefully hear and absorb the Word of God proclaimed in the first two readings, the Gospel and the homily. Perhaps if we are a bit exhausted after this half-hour or more of listening, something spiritually important has happened to us.

Third, we *give thanks and praise* in the Liturgy of the Eucharist. At the beginning of the Eucharistic Prayer the presider invites us, the assembly, to "lift up our hearts" and give God "thanks and praise." As the presider helps us remember and make present today the precious gift of Christ's suffering, death and resurrection, we, in turn, respond with one of the designated acclamations: "Christ has died, Christ is risen, Christ will come again," or, "By your cross and resurrection you have set us free; you are the Savior of the world." At the conclusion of the Eucharistic Prayer, at the great doxology (word of praise), "Through him, with him, in him," we acclaim the Great Amen: "Amen, Amen."

Fourth, in the *breaking and sharing* at the Last Supper Christ assured his disciples that he would be with them whenever they broke bread together and shared the common cup. As the priest breaks the loaf of bread in our sight at Mass, divides it among us and offers us the "wine poured out in our behalf," we receive Christ's gift extended throughout time and proclaim his death and resurrection until he comes again.

Our final action is *going forth* as a gathered assembly sent forth to be the body of Christ for each other and for a broken world. This is not the end, but rather the beginning, as we are missioned to share what we have received. If we have participated as earnestly as we can in these liturgical actions, perhaps we will feel a bit fatigued, but we will also know that by our actions we have participated in "that true Christian spirit" that is the aim of all good liturgy.

Communion Rite

Many of us who live and work in the high-speed, high-pressure world today will readily admit that one of the human activities that suffers the most is eating together. On the one hand, we do not particularly like or prefer eating alone, but on the other, because we are involved in so many daily activities, we sometimes have to simply "eat and run." Not good for digestion, obviously, or for the emotional peace of mind which meals taken together can provide. Unfortunately, our meals often turn out to be purely private affairs. We do not seem to have time for any other option. Most faithful Catholics take at least one meal together each week. We call it the Eucharist, the memorial supper that the Lord Jesus took with his disciples on the night before he died. Without doubt, this was a communal meal, the Passover that the Jews had celebrated for centuries and that we Christians continue to celebrate together in Christ's memory. The part of the Mass when we eat together is called the Communion rite. The word itself conveys the idea of doing something together as one. Unfortunately, however, for reasons lost in history, Catholics often think of Communion as their private moment with God. The fact that many others at Mass are also coming to the Table of the Lord along with us, eating and drinking with us, seems less important.

So, let us take a look at this rite we call Communion. It begins with the Lord's Prayer, in which we ask the Lord to "give us this day our daily bread." For Christians, this is pre-eminently the bread of the Eucharist. We also pray, of course, for bread for the world, a world in which millions go hungry each day (see the *General Instruction of the Roman Missal*, no. 81). Preceding our journey to the Table of the Lord, we greet one another with a sign of peace. In the early Church it was called a "holy kiss." It is not a secular greeting ("Hi, how are you") nor simply an opportunity to talk to those whom we might have missed on our way into church. It is not a duplication of the gathering rite. Indeed, it is not even our own peace we extend. No, this is the peace that only Christ can offer us as a free gift. In their letter, "The Challenge of Peace: God's Promise and Our Response," the U.S. bishops wrote: "We encourage every Catholic to make the sign of peace at Mass an authentic sign of our reconciliation with God and with one another. This sign of peace is also a visible sign of our commitment to work for peace as a Christian community."

After the sign of peace, the Eucharistic bread is broken in

what is called the fraction rite. We remember once again what the Lord Jesus did at the Last Supper: "He took the bread, said the blessing, broke the bread and gave it to his disciples, saying, 'Take this and eat it, all of you: This is my body which will be given up for you.' " Symbolically, this action of breaking speaks of our desire, even though we are many, to become one body in the Lord. While the priest is breaking the bread, the assembly sings a simple litany: "Lamb of God, you take away the sins of the world; have mercy on us."

After the priest's invitation—"Happy are those who are called to his supper"—the assembly approaches the Lord's Table. Ideally, at this time, we would sing a simple Communion refrain together that would speak of our communion, of our common union, of eating and drinking together. This is not a time for private prayer. It is a time to express our unity in the Lord by joining our voices in sung prayer. Once we have returned to our places from the table, we are invited to continue standing and singing our common thanksgiving together. It is also a sign of hospitality and respect for our sisters and brothers who are still at the table receiving Eucharist. After all have shared the Lord's Supper, there should be generous time devoted to silence and personal prayer.

The Communion rite ends with the prayer after Communion, which the priest prays in the name of all of us. Realistically, it may be true that "the world" will always impose on our daily meals. Having said that, however, it should be added that if we try to celebrate our Sunday meal, the Lord's meal, together as he celebrated it with his disciples, even our meals at home may become moments we can look forward to with a sense of eagerness and joy.

Need for Silence

A complaint that some Catholics have about the post-Vatican II liturgy is that it is noisy, that it does not afford them sufficient (or any) time for silent prayer. That observation is true, especially in ecclesial communities that are small and where most people know one another as neighbors. Often there is considerable conversation, greeting, or song rehearsal going on before Mass begins. This can truly be a source of distraction to those who simply want a few moments of quiet before or after Mass in order to talk to their God. There is already an excess of physical and emotional noise in our lives. Of all the places in our world where one ought to be able to experience the silence of the sacred, our churches ought to be foremost. Having said that, however, we need to add that our liturgy by its very nature and framework does include and demand certain moments of silence to be kept by the assembly. It is often only in stillness and silence that we are able to hear God's voice. Silence, therefore, is an integral part of every liturgy. It is called "sacred," for it is in this sort of silence that we are able to meet our God. What are these moments of silence we are invited to keep in the liturgy?

• *At the penitential rite*: After the opening greeting at the beginning of Mass, the presider invites each member of the assembly to call to mind our sins and reflect on our need for repentance. We need these few moments not only to put aside the distractions of the world from which we have just come but also to admit our unworthiness to enter God's presence.

• *At the opening prayer*: Several times during the Mass, the presider introduces a prayer with the invitation, "Let us pray."

The priest then pauses for a few moments so that each of us, individually and as a community, can have the opportunity to collect ourselves—body, mind and spirit—and add our own intentions to that of the presider. The presider then "collects" all our individual prayers into the one prayer that is then said aloud.

- *After the readings and the homily*: Once the Scripture lessons, the Gospel or the homily has been proclaimed, we are given a few moments to "let the words sink in," to take in more deeply what we have just heard.
- *After the Communion procession*: The last of the designated times for silence during Mass is after all have received Communion. As people are receiving the Body and Blood of Christ, we are asked to symbolize our unity as a Christian assembly by standing and singing together the Communion song. When all have received Communion, we have time to make our personal thanksgiving and to reflect on how we will return to the world to bring God's good news to all whom we may meet. Having said all this, it is obvious that the liturgy provides us times not only for "private silence" but especially the opportunity to pray together as a Christian assembly in "sacred silence."